JOHNNY CAN READ SO CAN JANE

Ruth B. Love

ADDISON-WESLEY PUBLISHING COMPANY
Menlo Park, California Reading, Massachusetts
London Amsterdam Don Mills, Ontario Sydney

Property of
John F. Kennedy
LIBRARY

*To
my late sister
Ida Love Barrington
whose love and friendship
served as a continual source
of inspiration*

Special appreciation goes to Cora Williams and Walter Loban for their valuable encouragement and assistance, and to Mary Claycomb and Lucy Blanton for editorial support.

This book is published by the Addison-Wesley Innovative Division.
Design: Roberta Holmes
Illustrations: Susan Nelson
Copyright © 1982 by Addison-Wesley Publishing Company, Inc.
All rights reserved. Printed in the United States of America.
Published simultaneously in Canada.

ABCDEF-ML-898765432
ISBN-0-201-04439-0

PREFACE

The prominent role of reading in daily life places a heavy responsibility on the school and the home. Parents, teachers, and administrators must do their part in preparing and enabling children to read.

Because of the amount of criticism directed at reading, and the body of evidence available on reading problems, I felt compelled to discover what is working and why. I used as a prime source the HEW report, *Programs that Work*, which identified a hundred effective reading programs throughout the country, and surveyed the teachers, administrators, specialists, and parents involved in these programs.

I attempted to determine why a particular program worked—whether it was the teacher, the specialist, the curriculum, the teaching techniques, the amount of time spent in reading, the role of parents, or some combination of these factors. In the last analysis it became apparent that the programs are only as effective as the people who implement them and that these people must include administrators and parents as well as teachers.

This book describes the findings from my study, as well as presenting additional information about other aspects of reading, such as how television viewing can be used in a positive way to promote reading instruction, and how to motivate children to read. The situations and the people are real, although real names are not used.

JOHNNY CAN READ—SO CAN JANE is written as a practical guide for the experienced teacher and the administrator as well as for the new teacher and the parent. Guidelines for parents are designed to provide useful suggestions to prepare and assist children in reading.

Finally, I have editorialized on some aspects of reading from years of experience in a field which cries out for help. If you gain one idea from this book, it will have been worth the effort for me.

CONTENTS

1 INTRODUCTION — 1

TEACHER SKILLS: *Motivating the Children* — 5

2 REASONS TO READ — 7
3 ALL CHILDREN CAN LEARN TO READ — 24
4 TV — AN AID TO READING — 48
5 TEACHING TEST-TAKING — 59

PARENT INVOLVEMENT: *Guidelines for Teachers* — 65

6 PARENTS AS PARTNERS — 67
7 SPECIFICALLY FOR PARENTS — 90
8 A SUMMARY OF READING APPROACHES AND METHODS — 99

ADMINISTRATIVE LEADERSHIP AND SUPPORT: *Factors for Success* — 107

9 ENSURING SUCCESSFUL READING PROGRAMS — 109
10 SCHOOLWIDE READING ASSESSMENT — 129
11 STANDARDS OF EXCELLENCE — 142

12 PROGRAMS AT WORK — 147

1
INTRODUCTION

Reading is indispensable—and enriching. In all aspects of human endeavor, whether social, political, professional, or personal, reading skills and habits are crucial. The prominent role of reading in daily life places a heavy responsibility upon schools and home. Behind every child who learns to read is a person who helped in that process. Frequently that person is a teacher or a parent.

The American public began to display anxieties about reading proficiency as far back as 1955, after the publication of Rudolf Flesch's *Why Johnny Can't Read*. The book raised doubts about the quality and quantity of education and ignited widespread debate. There was an emphatic call for educational reform intensified by the Soviet launching of the first Sputnik in 1957. In congressional hearing rooms and in classrooms the issues of education were discussed and dissected. Inadequate reading skills were the focal point of much of the criticism: schools were indicted for the extensive reading deficiencies among students of all ages.

Why Johnny Can't Read was reissued in 1966 and a new version came out in 1980, reflecting the fact that although many programs and approaches had been developed and implemented to meet the criticism, little had changed. Thousands of students still are leaving high school without adequate reading skills and are therefore unprepared for many jobs and to pursue additional training. There is no defense against that fact; nor against the fact that many more children should perform with increased reading competency.

Nevertheless a careful assessment indicates that today most children do learn to read and to read well, and that millions of children have profited from reading programs undertaken in the past decade.

One of the ways to correct the remaining shortcomings, to eliminate still existent miseducation and undereducation, is to appraise what makes a successful reading program and to share and use those elements as catalysts for further change.

This book's purpose is to do just that.

Successful reading programs are based on at least three major elements:

- **Teacher Skill**

Teacher expertise in teaching reading, coupled with the ability to motivate and stimulate students, is essential. In any method or programmatic design, teachers make the difference. Teacher attitudes and expectations set the tone for success. Teachers in successful programs know the difference between teaching reading and teaching students to read.

- **Parent Involvement**

Parents must be involved if children are to progress in reading. Involvement includes knowledge of classroom instruction and help at home. Underachieving children need extra time and reinforcement, and parents as well as siblings can offer such aid.

- **Administrative Leadership and Support**

Administrative support facilitates implementation of reading programs. Forceful, supportive leadership from principals can often be the key factor in programmatic success.

Each of these three elements will be addressed in following chapters. Chapters 2 through 5 discuss teacher skills: motivating students to read; understanding personality development and the psychology of learning; the technique of using television as an aid to reading; and the technique of teaching test-taking. Chapters 6 and 7 explore many levels of parent involvement and Chapter 8 summarizes various reading methodologies. Chapters 9, 10, and 11 discuss administrative support, both external (such as in planning and priorities) and internal (such as in strategies and materials), as well as assessment instruments and standards of excellence for reading programs. Finally, Chapter 12 is a compendium of successful reading programs now at work.

TEACHER SKILLS

2
REASONS TO READ

Desire is the fundamental impetus for most of life's successful activities. If a child wants to learn to read, that child is very likely going to do so. The key is to create the desire within the child, to motivate the child. There is no substitute for a child's motivation or desire to accomplish a task or learn something new. However, as one teacher put it, "Motivation is almost as individual as the student. You must try everything."

To understand the importance of motivation, we must remind ourselves from time to time of the various ways children express their insecurities. In an ungraded class of children achieving in the bottom quartile, the teacher, Ms. Handler, points up the varied behavioral patterns. "Almost all of the children may be described as discouraged, although this is shown in many ways. Some pretend they don't care; others have become the showoffs of the class to cover up; some act like the quiet mouse, hiding in some corner, hoping not to be called on by the teacher. Others are often in tears; some feign illness each time they can't solve a problem; some cut school or become pugnacious. Then there are those who become the daydreamers."

Ms. Handler, known for her high standards, goes on to say, "None of my children have been diagnosed as being mentally retarded or emotionally handicapped, but they are behind the class. They need help and love. What could be a greater challenge to a teacher? I have a wonderful job—children who need me, a place where I can have time and the privacy to find what their problems are, beautiful materials to help me solve and fill their education needs, time to *really get to know each one* of my children *as a person*, not just as a member of a group."

This teacher obviously loves children and enjoys teaching.

Motivation is such an influential ingredient in the child's developmental process that teachers need a clearer understanding of motivation and its ramifications in education. A brief review of the dimensions of motivation follows.

TYPES OF MOTIVATION

There are at least three types of motivation:

- **Fear motivation**—*a process which impels a person to act because he or she is fearful of the consequences.*

Mark is told to read for an hour every evening or he will be spanked. He knows his father means it, and therefore Mark begrudgingly reads. Though he is not comprehending much of what he reads, he is nevertheless reading, or rather pronouncing words.

Fear engenders anxieties and apprehension which often result in distinctive behavior. Instilling fear is not a way to develop in children a love for books or reading.

- **Incentive motivation**—*a process which promises rewards for performance.*

Deborah's teacher has a system of small rewards for children who improve in reading. The rewards may be a trip to the zoo, a special pen, or viewing a film. It may even be verbal recognition of reading performance on a given day. The class, clearly motivated, strives to make progress in reading.

Incentives and rewards are integral parts of our thought processes. We all desire recognition for our behavior. A pitfall in incentive motivation is the possibility of improving performance only for the actual reward. This type of motivation has limitations in that it is not intrinsic. The teacher is cautioned to keep the reward simple and clearly related to the action.

In the Discovery Through Reading program (see page 153), a fourth grade teacher commented, "By using positive verbal and intrinsic reinforcement, plus charting and graphing the students' work, the children have *proof* of their successes. Being successful turns them on."

- **Attitude motivation**—*the process of altering one's basic thinking toward his or her performance.*

Both Doris's teacher and mother have surrounded her with books relating to her interests. Doris's mother reinforces reading at home for thirty to forty minutes every weekday. The teacher, Ms. Barrington, has worked closely with Doris in helping her to understand that reading is not as difficult as Doris perceives.

Recognizing Doris's leadership ability, Ms. Barrington has given her more opportunity to work with several children in the area of mathematics, which is her strong subject. After several weeks of positive support, her attitude toward reading began to change. It took somewhat longer for Doris to be motivated to read independently, but as her ability to read improved, she demonstrated greater interest in reading.

In discussing motivation, one teacher indicated, "Most children are motivated to read through a recognition system that they understand. They love to hear and have others know that they are doing well. Positive reinforcement is the key. Heavy use of praise is essential to change attitudes and ultimately self-concepts. We all need to experience success."

Attitudinal change is difficult to accomplish. It is intrinsic and relies heavily on one's habits. Once the attitude is altered, the person has a greater chance of long-term or permanent change.

NINE STEPS IN READING MOTIVATION

In helping children learn to read, teachers face a two-fold challenge: (1) igniting a spark of interest in reading on the part of children who *can* read, but *do not* read; and (2) developing reading skills in children who have not learned to read, or who do not read well. Both are formidable challenges and require consistent and persistent motivational and teaching tools. There are many ways to induce children to read. The techniques require far more than employing reading methodologies. The interaction of an understanding of human behavior with instructional techniques is essential for progress.

These nine steps in reading motivation described in the following paragraphs establish a framework in which the act of reading can become a meaningful activity.

1. Communicate Reasons to Read

If children are to profit from the myriad of life's opportunities, they must be fully literate. There are always reasons to read, whether for information, inner joy, to gain new insights, or to explore the unknown. Children must understand this. The reasons should be communicated to them. Their purposes for reading have to relate to their world. Children, like adults, are more likely to be stimulated to attack even a difficult task if they see a logical reason for it. For example, David was obsessed with basketball and thought he wanted to be a basketball player. A sturdy well-coordinated third grader, David had not done well with reading. He was more interested in outdoor activities and pursued them vigorously. Little time was left for reading. Ms. McGillis selected several books on athletics, two of them about famous basketball stars. She shared these with David. The teacher also invited one of the high school players to drop by after school. His talk with the younger boy about playing on the team, as well as studying, made quite an impact on David. The desire to read began to develop. A lot of effort was required to assist David in becoming a reader. However, the first step was to initiate an interest.

2. Give Recognition for Progress

Children enjoy acknowledgment of a job well done. The continuance of progress can be greatly enhanced by overt recognition. The child should not only feel that the teacher recognizes progress, but also the progress should be publicly acknowledged. Peers, friends, and relatives are important to the child, and their knowledge of his or her progress can be extremely helpful. Classmates play a particular role. For example, Jonathan, a fourth grader, was well on his way to having a severely bruised ego, partially because of his difficulty with reading. His primary problem was remembering what he had read—comprehension. Jonathan could analyze words and pronounce them, but he had little ability to relate or recall what he read. When the teacher discovered his particular problem, she found an interesting book and asked him to read one paragraph. Then he was asked to paraphrase what he had read. Gradually, he could recite an interesting finding to the reading group. The mother's cooperation was enlisted, and both mother and teacher recorded his progress and indicated it to him. Jonathan's comprehension began to improve. One of the major reasons was the acknowledgement of his progress and the feeling of confidence which developed.

3. Offer Private Praise

Private praise is as potent as public acknowledgment in motivating children. There is hardly any substitute for the teacher quietly saying to a child, "You are now reading phrases, not just words. That's marvelous! It shows that you have studied very hard, and it is paying off. Soon you'll be reading all kinds of books. I am so proud of you." Almost any youngster will blossom under that kind of "stroking."

Private praise builds confidence and fosters interest in continued progress. Above all, praise for each achievement brings added successes.

4. Provide Tangible Rewards

An effective way to recognize progress is to give tangible rewards. No matter how small, children are usually excited about getting a prize. One teacher canvassed the neighborhood merchants and obtained a year's supply of small toys, books, pens, and other items for the achieving children. Another teacher had the class make different craft items which were to be used as prizes for progress. On a monthly basis the children helped to evaluate their progress and eagerly awaited the reward.

Caution should be exercised so as to avoid any temptation to work solely for the prize. The highest reward is improved reading. Stuart's father promised all three of his children $10 per week for progress in reading. The children worked frantically to memorize words and demonstrate their reading success. They were counting on $40 a month. At the end of the first month, Mr. Bolling paid out $120 to his three children. He noticed that they had long lists of words and even took them to bed. At the beginning of the second month, the parents received a note from Stuart's teacher suggesting that they work with him at home as she was doing at school. His reading was not improving significantly, although he seemed to have memorized certain words. Left to analyze a word, Stuart was lost. Then Mr. Bolling realized the problem. He talked with the teacher, and they began anew with smaller prizes. The teacher suggested trips to the zoo and the park and other types of rewards. There should be a transition from extrinsic rewards to intrinsic satisfaction with the act of reading itself.

5. Allow Independent Activities

Discovering and exploring for oneself is a basic need. Thus, a positive motivational technique can be providing an opportunity for independent study and exploration. Selecting books and other reading materials of their own is not merely an idle activity for students. They are making decisions and choices. A set of unfinished riddles, a series of word games, puzzles, repairing several toys—all are activities which can be pursued individually. One student spent six weeks (an hour or so each day) creating a reading game. When Dwight finally finished, he had developed a fairly complete word puzzle which the entire class enjoyed. The satisfaction derived from this activity was enormous and well worth the time involved. Cathy, interested in stories, listened on tape to her favorite stories until she was able to tell the stories to her reading group. Finally, she was asked to tell a story to the class.

6. Use Relevant Materials

A variety of reading materials, in terms of levels and types, adds to the excitement of developing the reading habit. Books, magazines, periodicals, newspapers, games, and charts represent some of the best resources available. Materials should relate to the diverse interests, cultural backgrounds, and learning styles of students. Ethel loves short stories and reads quickly. Large books and lengthy stories turn her off. Nathan finds auto mechanics magazines of top interest. Gary is intrigued with research, especially about foreign countries, and uses the reference books frequently. Stella enjoys the classified section of the newspaper because her family is in the market for a house.

The point is clear. As much variety as possible should be made available. Items need not be expensive. A bimonthly reading drive can accumulate many types of reading materials. The local newspaper would probably be pleased to get rid of day-old papers. Arrangement can be made for these to be delivered to school. Saturate the classroom with reading materials and allow children to select items of their choice. These acts alone can induce them to read.

7. Foster the Desire to Communicate

As we know, human beings have an innate desire to communicate. To commune with one's fellow humans leads us to reading. Speaking, writing, listening, and reading are intertwined. Teachers can help children read by demonstrating the connection between reading and writing, or reading and speaking. A fourth grade teacher involved her students in a major project of communication. They decided to produce a television talkshow. Each student searched his or her roots, wrote up the findings, and then appeared on the talkshow. The host learned something about each participant, but the guest on the show told about his or her heritage, with special emphasis on surprises. Each student prepared a book entitled *My Roots*. As the audience (class) listened to each guest on the talkshow, they thought of questions to ask and joined in the program. In addition to the research, students learned about the art of communication, especially via television.

Another class experimented for an entire day with NO READING. They could speak, write, listen; but no one was to read anything. This drastic activity culminated by having the class list the things they missed that day by not reading. Needless to say, the list was lengthy. They tried to determine what the world would be like without any reading. The experiment helped convince some children of the importance of reading in our daily lives.

8. Create the Urge to Know

Curiosity is one of the precious qualities of childhood. Children can be led to books through their drive for the unknown. Selection of books that satisfy their thirst for new adventures can create reading activities. Children can be convinced that books help them delve into the past, seek the mysterious, and travel to faraway places. In one classroom, the teacher featured different topical areas each month. For example, he selected books about intriguing countries, cities, and villages. The next month, books centered on science fiction. Still another month, the reading materials focused on unusual people in history. Children checked out these books for independent reading. They also took them home and were urged to do so. As they prepared book reports, their names were listed on the "Rare Book Chart."

In an attempt to create an urge to know or inquire, a third grade teacher asked the class to think for three minutes— about the two things they most wanted to know more about. Such topics as these emerged:

> How big is the earth?
> What is out in space?
> What is on the moon?
> How is rain made?
> How are babies born?
> Why do people have wars?
> What does the President do every day?

Why do we have Democrats and Republicans?
How do our eyes work?
Who is God?
Why are people prejudiced?
How were oceans formed?
How are tears made?
Why do some people hate others?

These were among the topics which formed the basis of "Reading Research." The class learned how to identify sources of data, how to take notes, and how to prepare a report. Children who had difficulty reading received special help from the teacher. She found books with simple vocabulary and conducted short reading lessons at the beginning of each Reading Research period. It was not surprising to observe the tenacity with which they approached their reading. Their curiosity was so strong that it aided them in skill development. Each child agreed to work on reading assignments at home, which reinforced the brief lessons at school, thus helping the children explore the unknown in their Reading Research projects.

9. Provide a Chance to Escape

Books offer children a wonderful opportunity to fantasize and escape momentarily from the world around them. The careful selection of books and stories dealing with intrigue and fantasy can stimulate children to read. Some children want to escape the misery of their lives, others enjoy pretending they are someone or something else. Still others engage in frequent fantasies as a relief from their world. Whatever their reason, children can be offered reading materials which carry them beyond the real world.

Ms. Jackson chose to read to the class immediately after

lunch. The children were enthralled with the unexpected, which seemed to occur daily as she read another chapter. Noticing the level of interest, Ms. Jackson asked the school librarian to collect books of fiction, and she sent the class to the library in small groups. They had fifteen minutes to pour over the small collection. Those who were unable to find a book of special interest went to the nearby public library. Each student eventually found his or her book of fantasy. Their assignment was threefold:

1. Enjoy reading the story.
2. Summarize the most "far-out" incident.
3. Make up a different ending for the book or write a substitute incident.

The children were excited about these assignments and eagerly worked on them.

ACTIVITIES FOR MOTIVATING STUDENTS

The motivation to read is inextricably bound with individual needs, whether recognized or generated. In other words, the desire to read can be learned, for it is not innate. Providing a good classroom atmosphere and climate in which children can grow and develop interest in reading is of paramount importance in the overall reading program. No program or method of reading instruction will do the job without close attention to motivation. The following activities are but a few of the techniques which teachers can use to turn their students on:

- **Storytellers**

In many communities, there are individuals who are adept in the art of storytelling. Invite such persons to join in a storytelling series. Such sessions can be followed by children reading and telling their own stories.

- **Roots**

Most children can be encouraged to explore their ancestry. Develop a process for doing so which might involve interviewing or writing about older members of one's family. These become very important documents of family history.

- **Sustained Silent Reading**

Persuade the entire school to set aside fifteen minutes a day for children to read anything they wish. The program is most effective if everyone in the school, and anyone who visits, joins in the activity.

- **Book Clubs**

Establish a classroom book club with specified criteria for membership. Children can assist in designating the number of books to be read for membership eligibility.

- **Book Drive and Auction**

Many families have children's books that can be collected

(for free) through an organized book drive. Newspaper articles about the drive can aid in soliciting books. Then hold an auction, using play money or real coins (depending upon the economic status of the children).

- **Authors**

    Have children write and publish their own books. A project to print and bind their own books can also be an excellent learning experience.

- **Reading Center**

    Establish in the classroom a corner for reading. The center could include books, magazines, newspapers, cassette tapes, listening machines, and other devices to promote reading. Children can take turns organizing the center as "Librarian of the Week."

- **Book Reviews**

    Establish a project on assessing books. Ask children to review the books they have read and share these objective reviews with the class.

- **Partnership Reading**

    Have children select reading partners for the purpose of reading to each other for a specified amount of time each day.

- **Play Writers and Readers**

    Use plays written by children or adults for drama. Emphasis should be placed upon trying to emphasize with the characters and playing the roles accordingly.

- **Teacher Reading**

    The teacher reads to the class a few minutes each day. He or she stops at a high point, leaving the children anxious for the next sequence.

- **Bookstore Unit**

    Arrange for the class to visit a bookstore with a wide diversity of books. Have the salesperson explain the different sections. Place particular emphasis on rare books and those of current topical interest to children.

- **Parent-Student Exchange**

    Urge parents to take turns daily reading to children and having their children read to them. Get away from the TV.

- **Interest Interviews**

    Develop with the class an interview form. Have children use these in ascertaining the types of books read by other children and by teachers. Interviews can be held at mutually convenient times.

- **Puppet Show**

    Use books and magazine stories for children to create their own puppet shows. Construction or collection of puppets and the development of puppet shows can excite students to read more about the characters. The students may desire to prepare their own puppet dramatization of a special book or event.

• Classroom Speakers

Designate areas of interest by the class and identify community persons to address the class on given topics. Prior to the visit, have children read about that particular subject.

• Using Drama to Stimulate Reading

Students of most ages enjoy plays and skits. Involve them in skits first—skits which are published and/or skits created around current events. These can be written by the teacher or by other children.

The teacher can obtain plays which students would enjoy performing, thereby enhancing their reading. Students in groups may be stimulated to perform plays. It is also exciting to attempt to have student-developed plays. These might center around their interests or experiences.

Have two students act out problem situations spontaneously. Such situations may be suggested by the class and would vary, depending on the age group. Some examples are (1) on a date, the young lady must be home in thirty minutes and the young man wants to stop for a snack; (2) your best friend stops speaking to you because she thought you told her secret; and (3) you lost a library book, and the teacher is unusually upset.

CONCLUSION

Motivating children to read involves discovering their underlying interests, desires, and needs. There is no one best way to teach a child to read. It may be subtle, overt, direct, or indirect. Observing children at work and at play can give good indications of their desires. When they are sold on the purpose and reasons for reading, when their desires and interests are stimulated, then reading becomes *the thing* to do.

3
ALL CHILDREN CAN LEARN TO READ

The task of teaching children to read is both paramount and possible. The challenge is to find the key to each child's learning process. Teaching children to read is not as easy as critics say, but neither is it as difficult as some would have us believe. Reading can be learned, and reading can be taught. But as learning is a continuous process, so is teaching—and teachers must continue to develop and refine skills in their quest for excellence. Teachers should remember that teaching children to read is quite different from teaching reading. When a teacher focuses on the subject of reading, the act of reading becomes an intellectual exercise. When teachers focus on teaching the child to read and build onto the child's enthusiasms, interests, and skills, reading becomes an enriching part of a world which holds greater promise of enjoyment and opportunity.

In our diverse, pluralistic nation, teachers need to know how to teach children from all strata of society to read. They must provide their students with the stimuli to ensure performance at the highest levels, for all students need guidance to expand their interests and broaden their horizons. Teachers must also be able to communicate with and relate to children from many ethnic groups, to children who are bilingual, and to children with a wide range of intellectual abilities. Some classrooms are as diverse as the one-room schoolhouses of the past. Relating to such diversity requires that teachers have an interest in human beings and what makes them tick. It also requires that they have a basic understanding of personality development and the psychology of learning. Teachers have to make each child in the classroom feel important. Discovering special interests, unique skills, and reading deficiencies is part of the process of extracting from each child his or her very best. We are not talking here about either miracle workers or magicians. But just as children learn to cope with differences, teachers must learn to handle diversity.

Most children, especially young children, have a passionate desire to read. For almost any preschooler the primary theme is "I want to read." Both the home and the school need to capture this thirst for reading, nurture and develop it, so that the joys and challenges of reading become part and parcel of the child's life. All teachers have witnessed children who enter kindergarten reading, or who pretend they can read, or who declare, "I am going to school to learn to read." For the latter group, reading and school are synonymous. Whether those children's interest is captured or unfulfilled depends upon the teacher—who holds the key to the important world of reading and communication.

CASE STUDIES

When confronted with a child handicapped by a reading deficiency, teachers ask themselves several questions: Why isn't the child reading? Is it a medical problem? Is it fear of failure? Is it lack of interest? Am I using the wrong method? What do the parents know about this? Does the book relate to the child's interests? What can I do? These searching questions are raised hundreds of times by teachers throughout the nation's classrooms. Answers are available. Teachers have some answers. Parents have other answers. Reading specialists have still other answers. Sharing these answers is one of the purposes of this book.

Teachers realize that problems of reading transcend economic, social, cultural, and ethnic backgrounds. We have witnessed numerous examples of children, from all walks of life, who were reluctant readers but who with support and assistance have been able to master the skills of reading difficulties. Possible ways to remedy them are described here. The cases illustrate that reading is more than the correct pronunciation of letters and words. They also reveal that psychological understandings are necessary to help the child cross the chasm from nonreader to reader.

Each case is at once encouraging, in that it exemplifies processes for diagnosing and correcting reading deficiencies, and informative, in that teaching strategies and techniques of human interaction are evident.

As teachers read and analyze the case studies, they will find themselves thinking of their own particular experiences with children. This is as it should be, for these examples are only illustrative of the dozens of cases teachers face daily. They also serve as pointers to larger issues which must be addressed: when children should begin to read, the screening and placement of children in special education classes, teaching limited or non-English-speaking children, communicating with and involving parents, creating positive classroom environment, handling discipline problems, knowing when to bring in the specialist, and motivating children to read.

Each teacher approaches problems and issues from his or her individual background of training and experience. Approaches will differ also, depending upon the resources in each school, each district, and each community.

Jamie Tolliver, Disappointed Kindergarten Student

Having reached her fifth birthday in May, Jamie spent the summer in anticipation of school. Not for a moment did she question whether her major task would be learning to read. Frequently she would use the terms *school* and *reading* synonymously.

After what appeared to be an eternity, the big day arrived. Jamie, filled with excitement, was delighted to respond to the teacher's request to tell her name, age, and how she spent the summer. As she later expressed to her mother, the first day was sort of confusing with meeting all the new children. However, her big disappointment, as she described it, was "the teacher didn't give me a book. I didn't learn to read." Reassuringly, her mother suggested she give the teacher more time. After all, it was only the first day.

Several days went by and Jamie's anxieties grew. She complained, "I am doing things I already know—counting, writing my name, and stuff." After several weeks, Jamie's mother began to notice a listlessness as the child prepared to go to school. Some sensitive probing revealed that Jamie's real anxieties centered around her inability to read and the lack of emphasis on reading at school. She lamented that she had no books and no one told her words. Again, trying to reassure her, Jamie's mother pointed out that learning letters and some words was the beginning of reading.

However, her mother sensed that Jamie's feelings were influencing her entire attitude toward school. She spoke with the teacher at length, and Ms. Richardson admitted she had noticed a difference in Jamie's outlook. Together, they began to develop ways of working with the child at home and at school.

First, they began to capture or recapture her imagination and interest through books. Multiple selections were available, and Jamie made good use of them. At home, the parent intensified her reading to Jamie and began having Jamie read to her. The child treasured those moments when her mother read to her. The teacher, Ms. Richardson, introduced simple sentences. Books about dolls, pets, and colors were used. Each day a few minutes were spent with Jamie and four other children, discussing words, phrases, and sentences. Remarkably, Jamie's attitude changed drastically. She began playing more with the other children. Indeed, a spark was ignited, and Jamie's former enthusiasm returned.

Jamie was especially fond of the picture flash cards with photos and sentences. She even made her own and subsequently developed a picture book. Her interest in reading was rekindled, and Jamie was reading second grade books by the end of kindergarten.

It was no surprise to anyone to learn that Jamie's intellectual ability was far above normal. The important point is that, through sensitivity and quick action by parent and teacher, a school casualty was prevented.

Conclusion

Children at any age are seriously affected when school does not meet their expectations. In the classroom, the sensitive teacher will tune into each child's needs and interests and devise activities to meet them. This can prevent psychological dropouts, that is, students who may be present physically but have tuned out the classroom activities.

Reading is such a universal desire on the part of children that teachers may want to rethink when it is taught in order to capitalize upon the all-important "teachable moment."

Miguel Reyes, Bilingual Fourth Grade Student

By the fourth grade Miguel had been in a class for the mentally retarded for a full two years. He started the year with an empty feeling which he was able to communicate to his teacher, Mr. Vitour. Mike's first male teacher established an almost instant rapport with the boy.

Mike was an average size for a fourth grader, with bright eyes and an inquiring mind. His English was somewhat broken, but his Spanish was superb—despite the fact that at school he was urged not to speak his native language. It was readily apparent that the youngster was not retarded but instead had limited English-speaking skills. In fact, Mike could read and write in Spanish, and enjoyed it.

Perhaps the fact that "they" thought he could not learn was the most devastating blow to him. Mike felt helpless to do anything about it. For two years now, Mike had easily performed most of the lessons in his special classes, with the exception of reading. However, he suffered terribly from the feeling of being misplaced as well as being considered "dumb." Hearing other children refer to him disparagingly was almost more than he could stand.

Consulting with the prior year's teacher, Mr. Vitour found that Mike had given up on reading and was now losing interest in other subjects. This was especially true during the last spring semester. He had become extreme in his behavior—it was either listless or aggressive. He rarely completed an assignment and became very hostile when pressed to do so.

The psychological damage was apparent to Mr. Vitour. After several discussions with the child, he decided to approach his parents. The Reyes family had immigrated to the United States from Mexico some five years before. The father knew enough English to get by, but the mother had quite a limited English vocabulary. Therefore, Spanish was the only language spoken at home. None of the six children used English very well.

The parents had high educational aspirations for their children, but they were becoming increasingly disappointed in schools. Discipline appeared to be very lax, and their children were not doing well in reading or mathematics.

The children seldom had homework. Of the four children in school, three were in some kind of special program, which the parents did not fully understand. They felt these classes were designed to help their children, although they confessed to no evidence of that.

After Mike's disenchantment was observed, he was referred by his teacher to the school psychologist. Much of Mike's problem stemmed from the label of "dummy class." He suffered, too, from unfamiliarity with the English language.

About the same time the pschologist learned that Mike could read in Spanish, the teacher began Spanish lessons three times a week. The children enjoyed the challenge and Mike and the other two students of Spanish-speaking backgrounds, were proud but puzzled by the sudden acceptability of "their language." Upon receiving a book written in Spanish, Mike's interest in reading sprouted like wildflowers. He treasured the book and read and reread it several times. What a feeling of satisfaction!

The teacher's problem now was to interest the boy in English. Mr. Vitour had decided from the beginning of the school year that Miguel did not belong in his special education class. He knew too well that he would never be able to convince the decisionmakers of Mike's normal ability as long as the boy was fluent in only one language. One day during consultation with the school principal, the teacher suggested an English class to be held after school or during the day— even at lunchtime. This was to be a class for all grade levels for any child who needed or desired help with the English language. They both agreed that such a class could probably serve as a model for the school district. Finally, it was agreed that scheduling the class during first period was appropriate. It would be an English language as well as a reading class. It was agreed that the principal would teach the first period for the teacher who volunteered to teach this unique class. By unanimous decision, Mr. Vitour was selected. He spoke some Spanish and had particular expertise in English, having learned English as a second language as a child when the family emigrated from Italy.

Parents of the children enrolled in the English class were encouraged to stress both languages. Some parents, especially mothers, began to come to school to sit in on the sessions.

Mike was absolutely thrilled with the turn of events, and his interest in school picked up considerably. By the latter part of the spring semester, Mike, with additional help from the psychologist, was able to be placed in a regular fourth grade class. While the boy deeply regretted leaving his friend and teacher, Mr. Vitour, he faced his new classmates with anticipation. He used the school library extensively and read a side variety of books about all kinds of animals.

By the end of the school year, Mike's interests and skill in reading had increased markedly. Reading became both a pleasure and a source of information. His competitive spirit returned, and he vowed to use his summer vacation to become the best fifth grade reader in the school.

Conclusion

Labeling children, especially with negative labels, can have a devastating impact on their behavior and performance. Undoing the mental and emotional damage is a painstaking process. Refined and frequent assessments in regular and special classes are imperative if schools are to be humane, educational institutions.

A foreign language is an asset which more children need. Since younger children tend to learn a second language with some ease, instituting foreign language instruction in elementary schools is a long overdue challenge.

Harold Mather, "Discipline Problem"

School problems were not new to Harold. They began when he was a second grader and intensified as he moved from one grade to the next.

He vividly recalled his teachers in elementary school pointing out that he was reading letters and words backward.

Since they did not appear to be in reverse to him, Harold could not understand this criticism of his reading. However, after repeated comments, coupled with laughter from the other children he became quite sensitive. By the fourth grade, Harold gave up reading, although he replaced it with other activities which gained even more attention.

Commonly referred to as a "discipline problem," Harold delighted in kicking chairs, tables, and people. When punished, he recommitted himself to getting even. It was true that some of his actions grew out of revenge. However, many times the teachers and his parents seemed to misinterpret his behavior—from Harold's point of view. For example, when he dropped a book or fell when running, these acts would be considered bad. No one seemed to recognize that his inadequate muscular coordination precipitated many such incidents.

During the middle of the fifth grade, Harold's school employed a psychologist with the use of special federal funds. Every one of the teachers seemed pleased, and Harold was the new staff member's first client.

After several discussions and some classroom and playground observations, Harold's parents were invited to school. They discovered that their son had a neurological problem and needed to see a specialist as well as a psychiatrist.

His parents also learned Harold's ailment was called a learning disability. They deeply resented the label but pursued the avenues suggested in order to help him.

Harold remembers well his year and a half of appointments with the psychiatrist. His parents and teacher began to react to him differently. His sixth grade teacher tried all kinds of reading materials until he found something that interested Harold. The story that finally caught his attention was a very sad story about a girl who was otracized. To Harold's amazement, he wanted very much to read that story. The teacher only told him part of the story, and Harold was anxious to finish it. The teacher, Mr. Day, was patient and helpful. Somehow, it wasn't as much of a struggle as Harold recalled from earlier years. In fact, he got through that one story and began to learn how to attack words independently. He wanted to read more. His desire grew into a craving for reading, perhaps because he had been unsuccessful for so long. As Harold received special, individualized help from a tutor, he began to realize what he was missing and worked hard to catch up.

Harold learned later that he had cost his parents lots of money. To him and to them it was worth it. By the end of the seventh grade, Harold was an avid reader.

Conclusion

All behavior is learned. In searching for the causes of extreme behavior, it is a wise teacher who knows when to refer the case to someone else. Discovering available community resources (that involve a fee or are free) to help children is a valuable ability for the principal or for an agency

Communication and joint effort with parents increase the chances of a child receiving the help needed in problematic situations. Many districts have obtained the assistance of volunteers to locate and compile sources. Psychological services for children are a wise use of talent, time, and resources in any community. City and county referral services are also frequently used.

Alex Wells, Embarrassed Sixth Grade Student

"Sixth grade is no grade to go to a reading center,"

thought Alex. He resented being sent there for the special help from reading specialists. In addition to being embarrassed, Alex was not especially interested in the academic part of school. After all, he had made it thus far without studying or doing homework. His teacher seemed to want everyone to read and speak as she did.

The reading center was located near the school library, and to his utter amazement, he found the unique equipment rather interesting. Alex liked mechanical objects and became fascinated with earphones, reading machines, and tape recorders. He remained uninterested in reading, however.

The reading teacher and specialist tried several techniques to interest Alex in reading, but to no avail. They consulted frequently with the classroom teacher.

One day his teacher, Ms. Frazier, observed Alex glancing through a book about athletes during the social studies period. He paused in several places. Ms. Frazier refrained from scolding him for not using the social studies book. She recalled that Alex's one success in school was in sports. He was superb in baseball and football and was well coordinated.

When Ms. Frazier discussed Alex's case with the reading center staff, they all decided to try an experiment. They persuaded one of the local, big athletes to visit the classroom and reading center once or twice a week. The exploration began by Ms. Frazier discussing with Alex the idea of meeting one of the athletes. He could not believe it. Even though his family lived in the city for years, they had never gone to one of the games at the stadium.

The teachers discovered Alex's favorite players and went after several players. It was not nearly as difficult as they thought. On the first approach, a football player agreed to visit the school and to talk with Alex specifically. Alex listened carefully to his hero and asked him many questions. Alex could not see the connection between sports and reading. Carefully, his new counselor explained why reading was important, and critical to getting ahead in life, even in sports. The star talked about the importance of reading when analyzing his contract with the league. Then he discussed how he used reading and math every day. Alex seemed to listen with a new ear. Alex's intellectual ability was clearly established as slightly above normal, although his grades did not reflect his ability.

As a start, every effort was made to find high-interest, low-vocabulary books. Newspapers and magazines were also available. Working on reading in the center for forty minutes a day as well as in the classroom, Alex made surprising progress. It did not take long for Alex to become interested in learning to read.

By the end of the school year, Alex was an average reader. Several other characteristics began to change. He started studying, even though it was hard to develop a routine for homework. School became more interesting. As his studies improved, his personality became somewhat more pleasant, and he developed a few friends outside the sports world.

Together with the football player, Alex helped in recruiting other big leaguers to volunteer at the school. In fact, the program became identified with the reading center. Interestingly, teachers noticed a remarkable improvement in school attendance and student behavior.

At long last, Alex's gigantic problem was being solved, and in the process he had learned several valuable lessons.

Conclusion

Children tend to dislike being singled out, especially for special help. A reading center or resource teacher program should be explained honestly to the entire class. Some teachers have found that allowing children to use the center for special projects as well as remedial help ends to remove the stigma.

Of course, most cities do not have big leagues teams, but schools can still help student discover local heroes who are doing something exciting or worthwhile. It will not always be easy to get their services, and in some instances, it may be necessary to expose the children to people they did not know existed—thereby creating heroes.

Carol Smith, Nonachieving Third Grade Student

Carol lived across the street from Markham School. She played on the playground before and after school. In fact, Carol was frequently at school. It was her source of recreation. She seemed to play more than work, her teacher observed.

Carol's pleasant personality caused her to make friends easily.

Ms. Austin enjoyed Carol but was quite concerned about her lack of progress in reading. The girl spent little time on reading, or on other subjects, for that matter. Carol would plead to be excused from oral reading and pretend to have a headache or some ailment.

The teacher reviewed again Carol's particular reading profile and found that she exhibited no facility for word recognition. She reviewed the Interest Inventory and found the girl to possess a wide variety of nonacademic interests, mainly games. Somewhat dismayed, Ms. Austin decided to telephone the parent. Now she recalled that Carol's parent had not visited the school. It seemed strange that she had met neither the mother nor father, nor even seen them across the street. The teacher's effort to set an appointment was futile.

Finally, Ms. Austin decided to accompany Carol home. As the children left, the teacher and child walked across the street. Ms. Smith was friendly, but nervous as she welcomed Carol's teacher. The teacher began to explain carefully that Carol was well adjusted, enjoyed her friends, but was clever at hiding the fact that she could not read. She went on to explain that Carol really made no attempt to learn to read and asked if the mother had noticed this behavior at home. Ms. Smith asked Carol to go outside, and she said, "We don't read much around here, but I want my children to know how to read and write." She went on, "I thought the girl was learning all of that in the school. Now, you tell me she can't read. What does she do all day? Goodness knows, I can't help her."

The teacher began to feel defensive because Ms. Smith seemed to expect the school to do everything. So she asked, "Why not both of us work with Carol? I'll get some special books and games and see if I can get her interested. That's the problem—getting her interested. Perhaps the games will help, since she likes to play. But I'll need your help, Ms. Smith. Could you read to her and maybe your other children for a few minutes after dinner? It would surely help, and you could get some books from the library around the corner. In fact, I could suggest several books, if you like." The teacher had not noticed the look of utter dismay on Ms. Smith's face. She seemed near tears.

Finally, Ms. Smith said, "I can't! I can't help her." As if talking to herself, she said, "I never did learn how to read." She began to sob. The story came forth. As one of the older children in a large family back in rural Tennessee, Ms. Smith attended school only part of the year. It was necessary for her to help earn money to feed and clothe her brothers and sisters. Just as she was about to get involved in studying, she would be absent for several days or weeks.

The sad story was one that the third grade teacher had not heard before, especially from a young parent in her early thirties. While she knew little about Tennessee or the South generally, she knew she must try to help. She promised Ms. Smith that she would think of some way to help and would visit her again soon.

After discussing the incident with the principal, they decided to approach the Adult Education Department. Ms. Austin knew that Carol would not receive any help at home unless the mother also received help. Fortunately, there was an opportunity class for adults who were functionally illiterate, but Ms. Smith would have to enroll right away. The class had met three times already.

Now the task was convincing the parent. There had been no indication that the mother had sought help. So, after school, Ms. Austin again visited the Smith household. Sure enough, Ms. Smith was fearful about joining a class. She had spent her life thus far hiding the fact that she could not read. Ms. Austin repeatedly made the point that the parent would not only benefit herself, but she could also help her children. Finally, the mother agreed to attend the class on Thursday evenings.

Ms. Austin, a very sensitive person, felt she should alert the opportunity class teacher, and so she telephoned him. After a discussion of the case, Mr. Howard suggested that he ask one of his other students to stop by for the new enrollee. As it turned out, this extra help was the deciding factor that evening, because Ms. Smith had lost the will to face this new situation.

However, Ms. Smith found other adults, some grandparents, very cordial. The teacher seemed to understand and gave her practical reading exercises. It wasn't as difficult as she thought it would be. After several sessions, Ms. Smith decided to discuss her experiences with her family. She suggested that they all help each other for an hour or so every day. At 7:00 p.m. in the Smith house, it was reading time. Carol got some much-needed assistance from her older brother, but the most important change was Carol's interest in reading. If her mother could go to school once a week and study every day, then she could learn, too. This was the beginning of a reading spurt for Carol.

Conclusion

We must never assume that the children in our schools or their parents come to us with homogeneous backgrounds. It is important to keep in mind that children in the United States come from every conceivable kind of geographical, ethnic, socio-economic, and psychological situation. In the case of Carol Smith, after a difficult moment when the teacher realized the child's mother couldn't read, some creative counseling and patience were able to help both mother and child.

WAYS TO USE THE CASE STUDIES

There are several ways the case studies may be helpful to teachers. A few of them are—
- Discuss in faculty meetings alternative ways of approaching the problems

- Identify one problem case in each class and design a method of handling it
- Contact community leaders to compile school-related resources
- Share diagnostic instruments, reading games, and other materials with other teachers
- Request that central office staff set up an interdisciplinary team to which children can be referred
- Develop a simple student profile card with strengths and weaknesses indicated
- Build a file of case studies and things that have worked for these children referral in future years.

TEACHER DO'S AND DON'TS FOR INDIVIDUALIZED INSTRUCTION

In today's diverse classroom, it is easy to become frustrated and demoralized, and thus resort to negativism when confronted with children with serious reading difficulties. The year is passing, and some of the children seem not to be progressing well. Parents are busy and TV is interfering. We must caution ourselves against the temptations of cynicism. Although we realize that negatives are self-defeating, both for the child and the teacher, they still can creep into classrooms. We know only too well that tact, positiveness, and praise can affect both the attitude and performance of children. It requires a great deal of effort and self-control for the teacher to rise above personal stresses to keep students interested and searching. Here then are some do's and don't. The don'ts are not characteristic of most teachers, but they can sound an alarm for today's instructors as they frantically individualize instruction for a diverse group of children in a large class.

Don't: "You have missed that same word four times today."

Do: "Let's try saying the word. Look at it carefully. How does it begin and end?"

Don't: "You are not paying attention. No wonder you are having problems."

Do: "Shall we read something else? This story doesn't appear to be interesting to you. What would you like to read today?"

Don't: "My goodness! You have mispronounced that word again. You must remember that this is *NOT* a Spanish class, and your accent is terrible."

Do: "It is fortunate that you can speak another language. Let's pronounce this word in English. Is there a similar word in Spanish?"

Don't: "Now, that is stupid! How are you ever going to learn to read when you give up so easily?"

Do: "Shall we try once more? It will get easier as we move along."

Don't: "When will you learn to listen? I can't repeat directions all day because you don't pay attention."

Do: "Someone forgot to listen carefully as I gave directions. That means you will not know how to follow up."

Don't: "I have told you again and again to do your homework. You're never going to make it with that attitude."

Do: "What happened? Did you forget your homework assignment? What can be done about it now? That assignment will help you with matching words, which we know you need to work on. What do you suggest?"

Don't: "Tell me, what are you using for brains? I have explained that paragraph three times. Either you aren't listening or you are stupid."

Do: "If you don't listen carefully, you will miss some very important directions. Without the directions you will not be able to complete the assignment. How about using your listening skills?"

Don't: "So you don't care! Well, if you don't want to learn to read, that's your problem. You're the one who will suffer, not me."

Do: "I don't believe you mean that. It is frustrating, though. Let's discuss reading for a minute. Why is it important? We use reading in so many ways . . .

Obviously the overwhelming majority of teachers would not fall into a pattern of impatience that produces these tactless comments. Yet all of us, at one time or another, may become discouraged and resort to varying degrees of insensitivity. Teachers realize that positiveness and praise, coupled with honesty, can offer children both insight and encouragement. They know also it is crucial for children to feel that the teacher understands the problems and will help with their solutions.

ACTIVITIES FOR PROMOTING STUDENT ACHIEVEMENT

- **Reading Corner**

    Establish a reading corner in the kindergarten room, complete with books, flash cards, and simple games. Allow each child to spend some time in the center daily.

- **Storytelling and Writing**

    Initiate a reading/language arts program based upon the experiences and interests of children. The teacher might begin by encouraging oral stories and writing them on large charts for reading. As these stories develop, individual books may be prepared with two or three of the child's own stories. Get parents and volunteers to assist with preparation of the individual books.

- **Tutoring**

    Develop a cross-age tutoring program using fifth and sixth graders to tutor younger children in reading and language. A variety of flash cards and word games may be used by the older students. Matching the tutor and the tutee is necessary so that a positive relationship can be established. A tutoring program can be daily or several times a week for periods of fifteen to thirty minutes. Weekly orientation sessions with the tutors are a way to help them assess and plan their activities. Tutoring can occur within the classroom or in other available space in the school. Research has shown that tutoring helps the tutor as well as the tutee.

- **Foreign Language Program**

    Many districts and schools are unable to finance a foreign language program. Therefore, initiating a program calls for creative staff-utilization, community resources, and student involvement. Here are some approaches which could be modified for a particular situation:

    —If preparation teachers with foreign language fluency are available, use them to develop a program.

    —Persuade a classroom teacher who is fluent in a language to teach a class for lower or upper elementary children. This could be held for thirty minutes before or after school or during lunch break. It might be feasible for another teacher to assume the language teacher's class in physical education or some other subject, thereby allowing time during the day for the foreign language class.

    Within most communities there are persons who speak a second language. Some are employed and others are not. The school might reach out to these community resources and involve them in volunteering for several hours per week. In the case of the employed, the business or agency might be persuaded to provide released time for the employee to offer this valuable service to the school.

    Some schools with specially funded projects, especially bilingual education, might be able to employ teacher aides with foreign language fluency. Here it is critical that the aide, like the teacher, possess adequacy in both languages.

- **Community Resource Guide**

    Recruit a team of volunteers to survey the community for the diverse agency and organizational resources available to children. The compilation of such a resource guide can help teachers and administrators to obtain assistance quickly.

• Children's Clinical Services

Urge the county hospitals and mental health centers to establish diagnostic and corrective services for children. It is a specialty which can be gratifying and prevent large expenditures and much heartache in future years.

• Use Folk Heroes

Identify the children's folk heroes in the community. Approach them, whether they be in sports, business, or in other occupations, and solicit their help in counseling and motivating children to read. A few minutes a day can be very helpful to the child who cannot or will not read.

• Study Center

Establish an afterschool study center staffed with college students. Persuade the college or university to give course credit to students who become tutors. Match the tutor with two tutees and provide a packet of material for them to use. The centers could be open daily, with children receiving an extra thirty minutes of reading assistance. The college's school of education could offer orientation and supervision to the tutors. Such an enriching activity can bring the resources of higher education to the public schools. Teachers would set criteria for children to participate, and progress profiles would be kept on each. The tutors could be instructed in assessing the mastery of specific skills.

- **Parent Education Classes**

Literacy or opportunity classes can be very important to the parents of children in low-income communities. School staff could work with the Depatment of Adult Education to establish such classes. Opportunity classes can focus on such job skills as driver's license tests, job applications, and recipes as well as on such family skills as reading to children, querying children after reading a paragraph, and jointly pronouncing words. Often these classes are more highly enrolled when they are conveniently located in the neighborhood.

CONCLUSION

Since 90 percent of all formal reading instruction occurs in the classroom, it rests with teachers to discover ways to solve the knotty problems related to reading. Working closely with parents and students, teachers can prevent and correct reading difficulties. There is no one method which works best, but knowledge of several approaches to reading is essential. Matching the approach to the child's needs in one of the most important steps in the reading process.

4
TV — AN AID TO READING

Television, without a doubt, has an indomitable influence on the lives of youth. Children are captivated from infancy by TV. By the age of three, children seem to be purposeful viewers of TV and begin to name their favorite programs. According to a recent study, children between the ages of two and five watch television over four hours every day, nearly thirty hours per week, fifteen hundred hours per year. Another study reveals that by the time a child enters first grade he or she has had six thousand hours of watching "the tube." This same TV saturation continues after the child enters school. It is estimated that by the time a student graduates from high school he or she has spent thirteen thousand hours in school—and sixteen thousand hours before a television set. This means that the average child spends over

30 percent more time watching television than in school.

Many educators consider television the enemy. The literature is replete with the effects of TV on education, especially reading. No one argues with the fact that children (and adults) spend an excessive amount of time passively watching television.

But television, whether we like it or not, is not going away.

The Challenges

Truly, one of the major challenges of this decade is to learn how to turn television into a viable teaching and learning tool for reinforcing and enhancing reading specifically and education generally. Traditionally, teachers have used outside sources and resources to enrich classroom instruction, to expose children to the unfamiliar. It is even more essential today for teachers to embrace nonclassroom resources.

A second challenge—and perhaps the most formidable one—is to reduce the exorbitant amount of time students spend as TV viewers. No matter how effective we become in using TV as a teaching device, it will never be advisable to have it usurp the majority of those precious hours of childhood. Television can never replace the joys of reading a book or the satisfaction of solving a difficult math problem or the enrichment from communicating and traveling.

The third challenge is for educators to make better use of commercial and instructional television. Children are passionately influenced by the thousands of hours they spend passively watching television. *In Introducing Children to Books via Television,* Pauline Gough points the way when she accurately says, "Ask any children's librarian which books rarely gather dust on the shelves, and one answer invariably will be, 'Books that are television related.' " This makes it clear that television has demontrated its ability to stimulate reading.

Teachers who capitalize on TV power can use it as a potent motivational teaching aid. Some of the ways teachers can make use of their "rival" are described in the following section.

READING ACTIVITIES USING TV

Using TV Scripts

There is something fascinating to students about reading scripts of television programs. In some cities, the audiovisual unit in the curriculum departments reproduce or videotape selected television programs after securing necessary permissions. The scripts are transcribed. In other areas, newspaper publishers print scripts for certain programs.

As students read the script as the program is shown, they make the connection between the printed and verbal words. There is a special intrigue, particularly with students who are experiencing some difficulty reading. Another variation is to have students review the scripts before seeing the programs on TV or video. Reading lessons can be developed with either approach. New words are isolated and discussed. Some teachers find that students increase their vocabulary at a faster rate when they are reading scripts and watching programs simultaneously. One teacher commented, "I was very surprised that substituing TV scripts for regular textbooks had such a profound impact on my fourth and fifth graders. There is something about the technical vocabulary, the dialogue, the quick pace that seems to intrigue the kids."

When Alex Haley's "Roots" was televised, newspapers provided scripts to schools in some communities. These were studied well in advance. By the time "Roots" was shown, the students in one district were highly motivated to read. Even the homework assignments became acceptable. One student, Harold, remarked, "I can't read so good, but I sure wanted to read 'Roots.' So, I got help and read the whole script. I learned lots of new words, but I learned lots of history too."

Selecting programs that will be educational requires planning and reviewing. The primary criterion is, Does it teach an important lesson to youth?

The Philadelphia TV project, one of the first in the United States, begins with helping students skim the script so that the characters and action can be introduced. One or two scenes may be acted out. New vocabulary words are placed on the board and discussed. This preparation for viewing heightens their interest, so that once the actual videotaped programs surfaces on the TV monitor, students are keenly interested. Some teachers vary the lessons by stopping the viewing at an appropriate place and discussing the key points, emphasizing facial expression and nonverbal communication, explaining an idiom, or underlining a crucial part of the program. In still other lessons, teachers review concepts in minilessons and develop special exercises to reinforce a skill. Many other enrichment exercises are devised to urge students to attempt creative communication independently. Some students write their own endings, develop a substitute scene, or even originate their own TV programs.

Motivation of students seems to be an immediate result of TV script programs. Obviously, this high level of motivation leads to improved reading skills. It also increases the amount of reading.

With the increased number of TV specials, adapted primarily from books of high quality, the scripts take on an even more significant role in reading. Many of the popular books are widely discussed, and students gain added status from their intimate knowledge of these important pieces of literature.

- **Introducing Books on TV**

    Book stores and libraries have attested to the rapid impact of television on book usage. Whether the book reviewed on TV is a classic, a new novel, or a primary grade book, children respond quickly. Television, which is readily accepted by children, can be used to lure students to bookshelves. Instructional television is now using its programs to ignite interest in books. In one district, twelve series on elementary books were presented in very exciting and interesting formats. When Mercer Mayer reviewed *Liza Lou*, the libraries were out of copies within two days. TV offers much more opportunity for dramatizing a situation. For example, storytelling requires preparation in order to be well done. Few teachers have the time to practice and develop the dramatic accoutrements necessary to sustain a storytelling series. Yet television can easily expedite such a series, complete with staging and flair. It should also be remembered that TV can employ professional storytellers, and these are brought right into the classroom. When the lovely book *Why Mosquitoes Buzz in People's Ears* was read in a special program, children throughout the primary grades in the entire city waited in long lines to get copies of the book.

    Whether on instructional or commercial TV, storytelling and book reviewing can introduce new knowledge and capture children's interests. Ms. McClanahan stated it well: "TV has become my dramatic aid in storytelling. It uses music, pantomime, puppets, and a well-modulated voice to do in seven minutes what would take me hours. So I use it to lead my children to bookshelves. Then I keep them there."

• **Developing TV Spots**

A few television stations have developed television spots that promote books as exciting and stimulating. These TV spots can indeed lead children to books, and ultimately to reading. In one community, in order to implement a program with the local TV channel it was necessary to get sponsors from large corporations. The corporations funded the program on an experimental basis. A sixty-second TV spot reviewing Dr. Seuss's *The Cat in the Hat* led second grader Joyce to obtain the book from the library. Truly, this one television spot caused her to read most of the Seuss books. She stated, "I could hardly wait to read *The Cat in the Hat*. Dr. Seuss's books are so funny. I really like them." There are very few TV spots which review books or turn children on to reading; but their possibilities are very real.

In another exciting program, upper elementary and junior high school students were trained to perform in their own television spots. These spots were designed to turn students on to reading. One class project involved answering the question, "What book influenced me most?" A series of sixty-second spots, graphically handled by students, focused on books which had had dramatic influences on the students. The series was popular, and children (the audience) responded almost wildly. To see their friends give an account of an exciting book made reading an almost natural consequence.

A variation of the TV spot idea is to sponsor prominent personalities who briefly discuss a particular book's influence. This can also stimulate children and adults to read. When one local folk hero discussed *Eleanor and Franklin*, both elementary and secondary students stormed the library. Even though the book was above the vocabulary level of elementary students, the children were so fascinated with the "story brief" that the principal was able to obtain a community storyteller to give excerpts from the book for grades four through six.

In planning a series of TV spots, the sponsor should be careful to include variety and different levels of difficulty.

- **Monitoring and Evaluating TV Programs**

One teacher found that assigning students to monitor certain programs and to evaluate program clarity was a good way of reducing the amount of time spent indiscriminately viewing television. This activity also was helpful in allowing students to assess programming. The monitoring activity was so successful that it grew to include students in all classes. All of the students were required to evaluate particular programs three nights a week. They received TV-related homework assignments. On the basis of the homework analysis, classrooms developed criteria for effective television programs. These criteria, in turn, were used by the students when they watched television.

The essence of utilizing the "electronic textbook" is to diminish its almost total exploitation of a student's time. Monitoring and evaluating also diminish the passivity with which most children view television, and help to open the students' minds to both the delights and the mysteries of reading.

• Student-Produced Shows

"Tune In" was a program produced by a group of sixth graders who became so interested in television that they formed a class after school. The teacher had special interest in TV and this class was part of an elective series of courses held after school three days a week. The primary purpose of the program was to get students to read. They thought of several ways this might occur; and these were some of their activities in this weekly thirty-minute show:

—*Story excerpts.* An especially intriguing portion of a story was selected, shared and left openended so that students wanted to read the whole story.

—*Authors.* Something particularly interesting about the author of a famous or popular book was discussed.

—*Can you imagine?* This series dealt with family stories, mysteries, and unbelievable sections of biographies.

—*The Book That Changed My Life.* Students discussed the impact of a book on them personally in this serious program.

—*Vocabulary contest.* This program was designed to see who recalled the most words from stories read. It was a kind of student "word bee" analogous to the spelling bee. All new words from prior lessons were used with entire classes of students. Two students served as teachers to test the word recognition game on television.

Test-Taking Skills

One group of teachers and the principal were able to persuade the local television station to use the public service time for a course on test-taking skills. They received help from the central office, and curriculum and evaluation specialists compiled a list of cogent skills necessary in taking several reading tests. These were then divided into lessons with one of the drama teachers presenting the TV lessons. The program was aired one evening a week, and students enrolled in the program. Every school in the district was flooded with materials. The daily newspapers helped to advertise the course. The PTA and other organizations became involved. Each month worksheets were distributed to the enrollees. This program was especially helpful to students in low socioeconomic areas, and it helped many middle-class students lower their test-taking anxieties.

• Technical Course

In establishing a course in operating video and television equipment, junior and senior high school students produced shows for their peers as well as elementary students. In preparation for productions much reading was necessary. Special reading lessons involved vocabulary, comprehension, and following directions. Some of their lessons involved explaining their course to elementary school children who in turn developed stronger technical vocabularies.

• Read Aloud Series

Oral reading can be spellbinding for young children. In an effort to encourage children to read orally, several schools were able to solicit prominent personalities in the community to read aloud to selected groups of students. On a weekly television program this series became part of the class reading program. It was *the* program of the week, and they looked forward to it.

A guessing game evolved around their anticipation of who would be the reader for the week. Interestingly, sports figures and politicians were their favorite personalities. Sporadically, the district was able to obtain the involvement of a national personality, such as a film star or singer. These were usually, although not exclusively, young persons who were familiar to the students. This added a special dimension. Evidence indicated a dramatic upsurge of interest in reading. Children frequently emulated the adults in the Read Aloud series. Ms. Barrington commented, "This series has made a significant difference in the children's oral reading. They try to imitate the personalities and really identify with them. Perhaps the greatest effect has been their improved pronounciations."

One student summarized his feelings this way: "Now that I watch the Read Aloud program, I read just like the baseball players. They read the best."

- ## Courses in TV

Some school districts are fortunate enough to own their own television channel and are therefore able to plan complete educational programs. One large school district established a special course in TV production, training students for credit to operate the camera and carry out all of the duties necessary for producing a show. A wide variety of programs were developed and aired. These related to many aspects of the curriculum—math, social science, music, art, science, physical fitness, and reading. One program of particular interest to students was "Word Magic" where all kinds of word analysis skills were demonstrated in cartoon fashion. Teachers found that children learned decoding and encoding skills from the program.

A senior high student produced a program of profiles of famous persons in history. Interestingly, younger students became quite interested because the stories were short and articulated well by the older student. Frequently, teachers followed up with an embellished story or provided biographies of the individuals.

CONCLUSION

As educators charged with the molding of young minds, with developing the citizens and leaders of tomorrow, we cannot afford to be pedantic or narrow. We must seek out ways to use technological advancements to provide youth with the best possible education. If in our search we find that television can assist us in helping students to master that most fundamental of all skills—reading—we are compelled to open our classrooms and our thinking. True, we must be careful and cautious; but if children spend more time with TV than with us, then we must help them use it with more directed educational benefit.

5
TEACHING TEST-TAKING

Test-taking is a skill as well as an assessment of knowledge. Teaching students to read is one important aspect of helping them to pass tests, but learning the skill of test-taking is also an essential step for students. If they—particularly those from economically deprived backgrounds—are to score well on tests, they must be taught how to take tests. Some would argue that teaching test-taking skills is synonymous with teaching the tests. But many teachers have found that the skills needed for performing well on tests can be taught effectively.

Preparing for Test-Taking

Most people are good at those activities they perform frequently. Therefore, practice at test-taking can enhance students skills. One fourth grade teacher found that the weekly test in reading substantially improved reading and test-taking ability in her students. These tests were designed to determine reading ability as well as specific testing skills. During the week, emphasis was placed on such skills as following directions, using key words, and answering multiple choice questions. In fact, as students read, especially during the reading period, they also practiced test-taking.

The testing climate has been shown to have a substantial influence on test results. Mr. Smith stated it well: "A stage must be set for children prior to giving a test. They should feel secure. I spend about fifteen minutes reviewing certain facts. Then we play a word game. The point is to relax the students and to show confdence in their abilities. It is also a very good idea to carefully explain how the tests are used."

In her third grade classroom, Ms. Estrada spent several periods during the week prior to giving the Cal Reading Test discussing how the test was developed. Each section was reviewed. Ms. Estroda said, "With confidence, my students learn all about the test." It is important to demystify tests. Children learn and perform best when they are not frightened.

Using Key Words

Using the technique of locating the key word in paragraphs or sentences is a useful skill in preparation for a test. In practice sessions Ms. Yarrow writes several questions on the board, and students are asked to find the key words in questions such as—

What is the *purpose* of solar energy?
Who is the *best known* civil rights leader?
How do you *feel* when someone hits you?
Why do *clouds* form in the sky?

After each such question, a paragraph follows. The answers are in the short passages. Students can then begin to write their own paragraphs, centering on a particular topic. Then they pose the questions. These are used in class discussions, and other students locate the key words. These reflect very helpful reading lessons as well as test-taking skills. Reading comprehension is the primary skill of reading which is strengthened by this technique.

Following Directions

Listening to and reading instructions are necessary skills for almost any test. As teachers practice these skills with students, they should be certain that directions are clear and appropriate. Here are some sample ways to increase clarity in following directions:

- —Read each line of words first. Then underline the words with the *ch* sound.
- —Say each word to yourself. Find the vowel in each word. Then draw a circle around each vowel.
- —Turn to page 6. Read all four lines. Say each word slowly to yourself. Think about the syllables as you say each word. Now read each word and write each syllable below the word.
- —These words have silent consonants. Read each word. Draw a line through the silent consonant.

Locating the Most Accurate Answer

Finding the most accurate answer involves several skills. For example, when testing for synonyms, the students need to know (a) the meaning of a word, (b) the word that means the same as the key word, and (c) the word that means the opposite. For example.

—Look at the underlined word. Read the three words below it. Which word means the same as the underlined word?

> He is a large boy.
> small
> big
> fast

Ms. Jones found that children enjoyed lessons of this type. After two lessons they could write sentences and make up their own tests. These tests were collected from the class and typed for further practice. A similar technique was used with antonyms.

Answering Followup Questions

Most reading tests involve using "word clues" from passages to answer specific questions. By using paragraphs in a basal reader or library book, a social science or science book, the skills of locating word clues can be developed and strengthened. Usually the tests will include a brief paragraph, followed by a question and multiple-choice answers. Ask students to read the questions and possible answers *first*. Then read the paragraph and locate the best answer. It is important for students to understand that by reading the questions first they will be better able to find the key word clues and answers.

Using Sentence Completion

As teachers know, there are a variety of ways that sentence completion can be used in reading preparation and followup. The following examples are appropriate for test-taking skills in most reading texts:

—*Angry* is the opposite of (1) offend, (2) happy, (3) irritate, (4) reject.

—*Inflate* is the same as (1) break, (2) pull, (3) expand, (4) stop.

—Someone who is *isolated* is (1) bad, (2) alone, (3) happy, (4) forceful.

—When the sun rises it is (1) dark, (2) raining, (3) dusk, (4) bright.

Reviewing Test Format

Many teachers review the various test formats in order to insure that students are familiar with them. Often children are hampered by the format itself, and thus their performance is affected negatively. Excerpts from tests for a different grade level can be used, or outdated tests are frequently available. Some teachers construct their own tests along the lines of the standardized instruments.

Mr. Richardson commented, "When I decided to give weekly reading tests to my fifth graders, I reviewed several tests. Each week I used a different section of the format so as to help the students feel comfortable with the designs. In fact, we discussed test formats and decided that some formats were more interesting than others. As the students ranked the formats which they preferred, the class decided to practice those sections which seemed most difficult. Homework was prepared and assigned in several test formats. Students began to improve not only in reading but in test-taking. I can honestly say that our average test scores improved by 20 to 30 percentile points."

Administering Tests

As mentioned earlier, setting the climate for testing is necessary for the optimum results. To the extent possible, administering parts of the test (if it is a long test) over several days rather than one one day can increase the chances of students' scoring higher. When students become tired or their attention span is diminished, accuracy is affected.

Urge students to skip (temporarily) those items which they are unable to answer. As they reread they may want to guess the answers. Remind them of the multiple choice test-taking skills which should be used as they proceed through a given test.

CONCLUSION

As teachers convey their confidence in students' ability to perform well on tests, and as they instruct them in the skills of test-taking, they are maximizing the opportunity of students to achieve well on these reading instruments. Further, teachers are helping students in developing skills that will aid them as they proceed through the educational process.

PARENT INVOLVEMENT

6
PARENTS AS PARTNERS

Clearly and historically, schools are a vital part of American communities. Beginning in the Massachusetts Bay Colony in the 1600s, continuing through the 1787 Northwest Ordinance, and up to the present time, Americans have demonstrated a faith in education as a way to improve the quality of life for both individuals and society. This special relationship in America between schools and the communities they seek to serve is predicated on the belief that parents have both the right and the responsibility to be involved with their children's education. Interestingly, as faith in education has diminished, the need for parental involvement has increased.

Wherever there is a successful program, it is likely strong parent participation exists. By far, one of the most significant aspects the government's Anti-Poverty Program was its opening of doors to adults who had been shut out. Their involvement has had tremendous impact on programs and on individuals. Education, probably more than other institutions, greatly benefits from meaningful participation of parents.

TEACHER ATTITUDES TOWARD PARENTS

If teachers are to help children achieve their maximum potential parental involvement is needed. Before looking at specific ways to enlist parent support and assistance a review of some of the philosophical and attitudinal aspects of parent involvement is useful. In the following sections are simple reminders to teachers of attitudes which help to include parents in educational processes and programs.

1. Assume Parent Interest

Teachers should give parents credit for being at least as interested in their children as they are. It matters not whether parents are low income or upper class: they are mothers and fathers. Teachers who remember this important information gain an understanding of the students and are better able to provide relevant education. It is wise to start with the assumption that most parents care deeply about their children. Most want for their children a better life than they experience. Assuming a positive attitude can affect the way teachers communicate with parents, verbally as well as nonverbally. Body language, the silent speech, can send stronger messages than actual words. A sudden busyness when someone appears, a glance away from the person's eyes, a disapproving nod—all of these are negative signals. They tend to exclude parents, just as defensive responses to pointed questions evoke caution on the part of the parents.

The teacher who acknowledges parent interest in their young ones will usually find students more positive and responsive. Even when interest is not displayed in the usual middle-class manner, do not assume limited parent interest. It may be that other priorities or problems take precedent over an expected action. For example, Joe's mother did not return to school with him, even though he had been suspended and the letter clearly requested that the parent accompany the boy to school for a conference with the principal and teacher. When he did not arrive with either parent, it was assumed that the parents were not concerned enough to work with the school. Frustration set in. Why didn't the mother telephone? Why didn't she write a note? Didn't she understand that her son was a behavior problem? How could anything be more important than finding out about her child's difficulties?

Upon further investigation, it was discovered that the mother worked at night and had instructed an older sister to accompany Joe to school. The sister's final choir practice was early that morning, and she was a half hour late reaching the elementary school. The teenager explained the situation, indicating that her mother would be there in the afternoon. What appeared to be lack of interest was really the pressure of other obligations.

When Joe's mother arrived at 2:30 p.m., she was most distressed to discover the number of incidents occurring at school. She regretted not being aware of these earlier. The teacher and parent agreed that the mother would visit the class once a week for several weeks (during the afternoon.) She would also monitor Joe's behavior more closely at home. The teacher agreed to telephone her if there were serious infractions of school or classroom rules. Joe was brought into the discussion and agreed to improve his behavior. After meeting the mother and sensing her concern and cooperation, the teacher began directing Joe's energies into different positive activities. His improvement was remarkable.

2. Show Respect for Parents

It is so very easy to generalize about parents, as though they are a homogeneous group. It is also easy to blame parents for the problems of their children. The difficulty with this kind of attitude is that is solves no problem. In fact, it establishes a barrier to communication.

There are dividends in getting to know the individual parents. Respecting parents as having a right to a set of ideals and ideas is often difficult, especially when those ideals are at variance with the school's ideals.

Regardless of similarities or differences, the teacher can get greater cooperation if parents feel they are appreciated and respected as human beings. Starting at this point, then, a relationship can develop. Mutual understandings can evolve.

Take the case of Paula's mother, Ms. Bailey. The mother had limited education, eighth grade to be exact. She did not speak with clarity and by habit tended to overdress and wear heavy makeup when visiting the school. Ms. Bailey was a proud woman, but she did not make friends easily. In fact, it was difficult to like her, as she gave the impression of being superficial. It was obvious that Paula was embarrassed by her mother's presence. The teacher's dilemma was how to move beyond the exterior and reach Ms. Bailey. She decided to invite Ms. Bailey for an afterschool conference, hoping to dissuade her from these drop-ins which mildly disrupted the class as the children stared and giggled. Ms. Matthew, the teacher, began to establish rapport by telling her how much she appreciated the parent's interest in her daughter. Ms. Matthew tried to learn as much as possible about the family lifestyle, particularly in relation to school. There was no homework or study period: the children were told to do their homework, but no place was arranged. As the teacher offered several suggestions, she noticed Ms. Bailey stiffened. The teacher continued, "Please don't be offended. I am merely sharing some of the things that have worked with other parents. Having a definite place and a time to study are very important. It need not be fancy. The kitchen table will do. If the television is off and a time is set for homework, your children may complain at first, but they will benefit." Ms. Bailey began to relax. She saw that the suggestions were not impossible. She also sensed the sincerity of the teacher. As they parted, the teacher shared a copy of a pamphlet entitled *Preparing for Your Parent-Teacher Conference*. This one meeting was the beginning of a long relationship. The mother left feeling important and able to help her children in some ways.

Parents, even in this age of criticism, want and need the respect of teachers. Respect is expressed in many ways, but most individuals would like their opinion to be heard and to feel that they are important.

3. Be Positive and Supportive

One of the frequent complaints from parents is that they are invited to school only when there is a problem. It is a fact that we need parents' help when trouble arises; but we also need them to prevent problems. It is amazing how a positive attitude toward parents generates a similar response. The teacher's interest and enthusiasm are readily apparent. When parents feel there is a special interest in their child, a door is open for wider communication. Both parent and teacher need support from each other. As teachers reach out to parents, this positive approach conveys our confidence in them as responsible individuals. For example, Mr. Patterson came to school early one morning to "set the teacher straight." He was certain that Ms. Fowler disliked his daughter Mary. His conviction grew out of Mary's reluctance to attend school. It was a struggle every day to get her to leave home. In an abrasive manner, Mr. Patterson approached the teacher in the hallway with, "Why don't you like Mary? You have caused her to hate school. I want her transferred to another room right now." Ms. Fowler listened and invited Mr. Patterson inside the classroom. She responded that she was sorry he felt that way. She explained, "Actually, Mary is a very pleasant girl. However, she is having some difficulty with her reading. She sees letters and words in reverse, and I have asked for her to be tested. I am sorry that none of my letters to you were answered." Mr. Patterson was startled. He had not received any letters. Neither had his wife. There must be some mistake. He calmed down and began to ask questions. Ms. Fowler also inquired about Mary's reading habits at home. She discovered that the girl never picked up a book or a magazine. Mr. Patterson acknowledged that he and Ms. Patterson were concerned about her complete lack of interest in reading. They had no idea of the reversal problem. After some discussion, both agreed that perhaps Mary's reluctance to attend school was due to her frustrations with reading and mathematics. He agreed to be as helpful as possible. Both parents would come back to school as soon as the tests were completed.

4. Communicate Standards and Expectations

If parents are to be involved in the program, they need to be informed about the standards, objectives, goals, strategies, and materials. At the beginning of the school year, an orientation meeting could serve this very useful purpose. When parents clearly understand what their second grader is expected to learn during the year, when they are aware of the books he or she is expected to read, when they see the level of his or her reading early in the year, then, and only then, can they fully appreciate the dimensions of the efforts necessary to reinforce and assist.

The orientation meeting requires planning so as to give both a general overview of the reading plans for the year and a written status report on each child. Included in the meeting should be some discussion as to parents' role in helping their chldren.

GUIDELINES FOR INVOLVING PARENTS IN READING

Parents are the children's first teacher. They know more about their children than any other person. This can be a valuable resource. Seize every possible opportunity to engage them in the reading program. Teachers have tried many approaches to parental involvement. Some approaches work with certain parents and fail with others. There are, however, some guidelines which have been tested and found to be effective. Those that follow relate specifically to reading, and teachers can adapt them to their situation, personality, and needs. They represent only a few of the ways in which parents can be stimulated to act on behalf of their children.

1. Develop an Outreach

Do not take for granted that parents feel welcome in the classroom. It is even less certain that they feel comfortable with the reading program. For years, we have debated whether to seek parental help in teaching reading. There remains confusion in the minds of some, although the confusion in recent years has been somewhat ameliorated.

An outreach program designed to solicit parent assistance in reading activities is imperative. The approach should be personal, either through a letter, a telephone call, or a visit. A plea for help is difficult to reject, especially if the need is established. If the parent learns that his or her child will benefit, even when there is no major problem, that parent is quite likely to respond positively. Once the parent is assured of the need for his or her involvement, the task becomes one of specificity and results.

Mr. Oliver met with much enthusiasm when he wrote to each parent and then telephoned them. The meeting was scheduled for the evening, for the distinct purpose of discussing "Reading Problems and Solutions—Your Child and You." He began by giving the overall status of the class. Parents were alarmed to learn that the average fourth grader was at least two years below grade level. Then he shared the individual student profiles with the respective parents. He made a point of indicating that each of the children had the ability to improve substantially. As Mr. Oliver discussed some of the reasons why reading deficiencies occur, parents became quite animated, and the discussion was most productive. Of course, the obvious question was, "What can we do?" Mr. Oliver put forth his proposal: he requested a monthly meeting of parents to rally behind the reading program, to share problems and progress. Second, he asked the parents each to spend one hour for five nights a week in helping their youngsters with reading. Third, Mr. Oliver agreed to hold individual conferences with each parent to discuss the particular types of activities appropriate for the child involved. Finally, the teacher pointed out that he would assign homework that related to the reading lessons and asked the parents to monitor the completion of the homework. As he explained the student profile cards, parents realized they could readily keep track of their child's performance. The meeting was a success, and the schedule continued for the rest of the school year. As children improved, parents became increasingly involved. Some of the parents began to meet on weekends to take their children to special events in the community. The monthly meetings were a combination of how to teach reading and show-and-tell. Difficulties were openly discussed and suggestions made.

In the meantime, Mr. Oliver's instructional program changed. He gave much more attention to prescriptions for individual reading needs. The library was used more frequently for independent study. Reading projects in which students sought answers to major questions were established each month. Some of the questions were—

Can human beings be fed from undersea plants? How?

Who was Madame Curie and what did she give to the world?
Why was Jackie Robinson revered?
What makes rain?
What route did Christopher Columbus take to America?

Students read hard to find the responses to at least one puzzling question. A written report was prepared and shared with the class. Each child was permitted to join the "Researcher's Club" which stimulated further interest in reading to discover answers. This approach involved extra time and effort by the teacher and parents, but the rewards were gratifying. By the end of the school year, all but two students were at or above grade level in reading.

2. Establish an Advisory Committee

Involving parents in the implementation of the program is essential. Many teachers have established an advisory committee of parents. These parents assume responsibility for supporting the reading program. During monthly meetings, they review the status of objectives, student progress, and areas needing improvement. The committee also seeks resources that can benefit the program. One of the activities is to communicate with other parents and community representatives. Interpreting programs to the community is a massive job, and each committee member is charged with that task. Such a committee can offer advice for consideration in modifying aspects of the program. Parents can be excellent recruiters of parents. An advisory committee can substantially expand parent involvement.

Guidelines for the committee can be developed prior to its

operation. With a rotational membership, a variety of parents have the opportunity to serve.

3. Make Home Visits

While home visitations are out of fashion in many communities, nevertheless a visit from a teacher is still one of the most effective ways of reaching parents. First, the teacher is on the parents' turf, and all of us tend to be more at ease in familiar surroundings. Second, the teachers interest in their child is expressed or measured in terms of the extra effort made to visit and consult with the parents. Third, being in the child's home expands the teacher's knowledge and understanding of the child, thus aiding in the teaching-learning process.

With all of the additional responsibilities, home visitation seems like one more activity; but teachers may be assured that parents usually respond warmly to this level of effort. It may be possible to make two visits per week in one afternoon. It may be possible to get the principal to schedule a minimum day, allowing for home visitation. Some teachers have even scheduled an appointment at lunchtime, meeting with employed parents at their home. Still others have found that evenings are the only convenient time to confer with working parents in this homes. Even though an extraordinary effort is required, the ultimate benefit to the child has proved to be worth it. In some schools, with the use of state or federal funds overtime provisions are made, and teachers are remunerated for evening meetings. In other schools, the community assistants assume responsibility for parent contacts and make home visits. In still other situations, substitutes are employed to replace teachers for partial-day home visits. The teacher-parent contact should take priority over other forms of communication and is most effective.

4. Hold Individual Conferences

Parent-teacher conferences are part of public school practices. It is a practice which has long endured. Successful parent-teacher conferences require effort by teachers and parents. In preparing for the conference, some teachers have found the following suggestions helpful:
- Plan the conference at a time convenient for working parents.
- Start the discussion on a positive note. Stress the strength of the child first.
- Sit in a chair away from your desk in order to create a conversational tone.
- Put parents at ease by asking them to share their observations about their child.
- Discuss the records, profile, and progress.
- Specify the reading difficulties and successes and why you think they are occurring.
- Request assistance from parents.
- Use plain language.
- Ask parents for suggestions.
- Reach joint agreement on what should be worked on by each of you. Be specific.

5. Include Parents in Program Planning

As schools and classroom personnel begin a reassessment of reading programs, a planning committee which includes parents is a desirable way to proceed. Parents are able to provide the kind of insights about their children that could be overlooked in our search for methodologies and materials.

If parents are familiar with the reading goals, objectives, and strategies, they are motivated to assist in implementation.

The faculty at Washington School in a large city decided to plan a new direction in reading. At the end of the school year, they were discouraged with the test results, the attitude of the children, and the poor parent participation. Though demoralized, they decided to analyze the program on a schoolwide basis. These were their findings:

—The principal and vice-principal were occupied with discipline, meetings at the district office, parent complaints, and paperwork. There was too little time spent on reading or any other instructional area.

—Within the school, some eighteen different reading approaches were used, and these were based on various published textbooks rather than on a decisive method determined by the teacher. Within a given grade, three to four sets of textbooks were used.

—Because these approaches varied considerably, there was minimal continuity. In other words, the books defined the method when they should have been used to facilitate, through a series of discrete methods, the teaching of reading.

—Most of the parents worked, and others received some type of social welfare aid. The result was almost no direct involvement in the reading activities.

—Children seldom completed homework, and therefore teachers decreased the frequency and amount given.

The end result of these and other circumstances was poor performance. On standardized tests, the children scored from two to four grades below their respective grade levels. On criterion-referenced tests, the results were hardly better. After nine months of hard work they were demoralized, discouraged, and really dismayed. Last year, the school had received over $200,000 in federal funds, and they had hired teacher aides to assist in reading.

It was agreed that a special meeting of parents and teachers should be called. It was a crisis alarm. Several forms of communication were used—letters, telephone calls, radio, and home visits. The response was encouraging.

The principal began the meeting by summarizing the dismal reading levels and some of the reasons for them. He then asked parents for their comments. The staff members were surprised to hear parents criticize themselves as well as the school. "Parents aren't taking time with the kids," "We are buying candy instead of books," "How many of us really help the children read at night?" "Some of us don't even know where the kids go after school." Other comments: "There isn't enough time spent on reading at school." "The aide is not the teacher, and every day she teaches my kid. He has no time with the teacher." "These books—the children don't seem to like them—they say the stories are silly."

Then parents and teachers were asked to make recommendations for tackling the problems. A teacher summarized these on the chalkboard:

—Review what we are now doing. What reading methods are used? Develop a school reading program with definite methods of teaching reading. Limit the methods to two approaches, one for primary and one for upper grades. Establish a fifteen-member planning committee of teachers and parents who would obtain ideas from the larger group.

—Appoint a team of teachers, parents, librarians, and aides to select the textbooks to be used. Select one set for primary and one for upper grades. Everyone will use the selected textbooks, but they may supplement with any books they desire.

—Give homework in reading for four nights a week— Monday through Thursday.

—Parents should help their child for at least thirty minutes every night. Ten minutes should be spent reading to or listening to the child read.

—A record of each child's progress or lack of progress should be kept. Monthly meetings should be held at school and the child's chart should be discussed.

—During the summer, children should be encouraged to attend summer school, use the library, and read as much as possible.

The program started in September, after several planning sessions during summer vacations. A training program was held for the aides, specifically focused on reading. Teachers attended workshops and classes related to reading. Special attention was given to motivating children to read. Prior to the beginning of school, parents attended a series of meetings that dealt with reading instruction at home. Games were made, techniques discussed, books displayed, and in general, parents received information on reading.

The year began with the school and parents turned on to reading. They adhered to their plans. At midyear, they scheduled a special evaluation meeting to assess how the children were doing. This meant that a midyear test had to be given. With some of their federal funds, the program planning committee recommended that tests be purchased, given, and scored. The results reported by the consultant were very revealing. Some children had made significant progress; others lagged. The parents and teacher made some modifications and intensified their efforts. For example, an afterschool tutoring program was established for students with special difficulties. Community volunteers were recruited to staff the tutoring program.

By year's end, Washington School staff, parents, and children were proud of their progress. They decided to continue another year.

The key point here is the level and degree of parental involvement. Parents were informed about the problem and engaged in the solutions. When a parent became somewhat lax, he or she was visited and urged to continue. Overall, parents and teachers cooperated well. Teachers felt better about themselves as educators. Parents felt better about themselves as parents. Children certainly felt better about themselves as students. In fact, not only were they feeling better, they were performing better.

6. Establish Education Programs for Parents

Some parents can be enticed to become involved through their own educational experiences. Parent education classes, designed to meet specific needs and interests of parents, have increased parental support of elementary and secondary education.

There are several types of classes that can be beneficial to adults and subsequently to their children. Here are a few examples: a class for parents of infants and preschoolers; classes on how to help young children read, on how to assist slow readers, on how to recognize and combat dyslexia, and on how to select children's books; and classes on reading around the house and on storytelling.

7. Solicit Parent Feedback

The insights which parents bring to the reading program can be helpful in evaluating the overall program as well as in assisting the individual child. When parents are asked to comment on the program, they either know from experience something about it, or they have perceptions about it. In either case, listening to their positive and negative statements is an important aspect of assessment. If parents are uninvolved, they are more likely to be negative. This is especially true if their child is not reading well.

For example, several groups of parents were asked to comment on effective reading programs in their schools. Specifically, they were asked *why* the program succeeded. Some teachers surveyed parents; others scheduled brainstorming meetings; still others held individual conferences. Parent perceptions and comments were as follows:

- —"The teacher made me feel important."
- —"I have seen a great improvement in our daughter's reading ability since she has been in the program."
- —"I now help my child at home, and I have learned how to do it."
- —"My own skills have impoved."
- —"The program is our program because we helped to plan it."
- —"For once, parents were welcome and included in all aspects of the program."
- —"The teachers love what they are doing, and the children feel important."

—"Our program emphasizes parent orientation, so as parents we are constantly aware of our children's progress as well as their weaknesses."
—"The principal and teachers ask our opinion."
—"The teachers help us understand how to help our children."
—"Parents and teachers work as a team.
—"Our teachers have learned some things from us."
—"The children feel that the school and home are there to help them."
—"Parents can do more than babysit."
—"Keeps parents involved and aware."

Teachers should bear in mind that these comments came from parents who were familiar with the program objectives and activities. They were equally aware of their children's problems and progress. The sense of program ownership which was expressed gives credence to the notion that being involved means having a role to play and an opportunity to contribute to the success of the program.

8. Urge Classroom Observation

Parents who visit classes are obviously more informed about activities generally, and reading specifically. The classroom can be a laboratory for children where parents observe the experiments. Helping parents understand what to look for during the reading sessions can expand their perceptions and thus cause the visits to be enriched.

One teacher prepared these cues for parents:
—Give particular attention to your child's interaction with others in the reading group. Is he or she accepted? Where does he or she sit?

—Notice the length of time your child remains interested in the story. Does he or she begin to glance at other things? Is he or she intrigued by the story? How long can he or she sit still?
—Does your child recall all or part of what was read?
—Can your child separate words into syllables? Can he or she sound out words? Does he or she understand consonants and vowels?
—Does your child volunteer to answer a question or write something on the board?
—During the followup period, does your child complete the assignment?
—In independent study, what does your child select to do? Does he or she read, listen to stories, draw, talk? What kind of books or magazines does he or she choose?
—Does your child listen to instructions? Does he or she follow the instructions?
—When reading aloud, does your child miss many words? How does he or she react when words are mispronounced and corrected?

The parents appreciated the cues and added some of their own. They felt the questions helped them zero in on reading and their child's interaction with the process.

Chairs should be available for parents to use. This little convenience signals a welcome and expectation of their visit. Teachers may need to discourage children from talking with the parent during the reading lessons, and encourage parent observation. There are always a few minutes during recess for discussion. Teachers may want to request the parent to give them some feedback on their observations. During this time, it may be helpful to suggest one or two specific actions a parent might take to assist the child—and make sure they are *specific* actions because it is not too helpful for teachers to say, "Help your child with reading." Many parents would take that to mean listen to the child read and correct the mistakes. Teachers will want parents to assist in specific ways.

9. Request Assistance in Reading Support

It takes a great deal of action and activity to support a reading program. Teachers need parents to help with a number of reading related activities. These can include the following:

—Selecting textbooks, using the criteria developed jointly by teachers, parents, librarians, and curriculum specialists, provide useful insights to parents.
—Monitoring test taking is another area where parents can assist and learn more about testing.
—Correcting tests (non-standardized) gives a parent an overall picture of relevant questions in reading.
—Selecting library books, sharing interesting books, and returning them also provides meaningful information to the parent.
—Traveling with and supervising students on field trips is a common practice. Involving parents in the instructional preparation and followup is another dimension.
—Encouraging parents to present their special talents and skills to the class, such as in art, music, dance, and ethnic cooking, enriches instruction.

There are many other day-to-day activities in which parents can be involved. Use every opportunity to get and keep their attention.

10. Encourage Parent-Sponsored Projects

Parents, as representatives of the community, can be resourceful agents. They possess diverse skills and talents which can benefit the school and the children. Discover and use these resourceful persons. Following are examples of some special projects which have directly aided reading programs:

—*Book fair.* Parents in a small community sponsored a book fair to supplement the modest library. They sought children's books from their employers, colleagues, and friends. These were displayed in the auditorium with each parent committee member assuming responsibility for different categories of books. Classes visited the book fair and wrote the names of the books that interested them. The books were given to the school library after they were properly labeled and catalogued.

—*Storytelling.* In most communities there are people who are artists in storytelling. A group of parents sought out their storytellers, many of whom were older citizens. They arranged for them to visit classes on a regular schedule. The children were fascinated with this project. The demand exceeded the supply. The parents decided to initiate a class on storytelling. They urged other parents to attend. The instructors were the "master storytellers" who were already involved. Some of the children became interested, and during the third year of the project they established a miniseries on storytelling for children in grades four through six.

11. Encourage Volunteer Tutoring

In a community with several large industries and two major universities, the parents conceived the idea of establishing tutoring centers at local churches, recreation centers, and some schools. They recruited persons who were not employed to join the project. A teacher volunteered to provide the orientation for tutors. Another teacher collected tutoring guides and pertinent materials. After consulting with the staff, several kinds of tutoring programs were established. One program operated during the school day when students were scheduled out of class for thirty to forty minutes daily. Another program operated immediately after school at the school site. The third program operated at several churches in the evening. Fifth and sixth graders were encouraged to attend.

The volunteer tutoring program grew into a districtwide program, first staffed by volunteer parents and later by a paid staff. Periodic workshops were held and reading instruction received quite a boost.

12. Utilize Parents as a Classroom Resource

One very active parent noticed the wide variety of hobbies practiced in the community. She was inspired to try to share these hobbies and talents with the children in the school. Ms. Branch discussed her idea with her child's teacher, and they agreed to test the idea in one classroom first. The teacher suggested that bringing speakers into the classroom could stimulate children to read. Ms. Branch was able to identify thirty persons with interesting hobbies. She obtained commitments from seventeen of these individuals. They agreed to bring their materials or invite the class to visit their homes. Some of the hobbies were modern day activities such as designing transistors; others were almost lost arts, such as quiltmaking, canning, and preserving foods.

The stimulation for reading was beyond expectations. Class projects and individual projects developed from the use of these valuable resource persons. The program spread throughout the entire school. The original parents were able to expand their group. It became one of the most widely discussed activities in the district. The impact on reading has been profound. Children have eagerly pursued additional information. They have written their own books and reports.

CONCLUSION

We know the importance of parents in creating a desire for learning. Parents are critical partners in the reading program. Parents also view teachers as critical partners. Without a doubt, parents see the teacher and his or her skills as the most important reason for reading success. Teaching reading and communicating with children are perceived by parents as major ingredients in school programs. These perceptions speak to both the expectations and the faith which parents have in teachers. If a cooperative relationship is to exist, there must be mutual respect and understanding of the roles each person should play in helping the child. One parent said it this way: "My boy's teacher was the key that unlocked the door of reading. She knew him. She liked him. She taught him."

7
SPECIFICALLY FOR PARENTS

Within most school districts and communities, there are "How-To" manuals for parents. The usual manual reflects ideas from teachers, librarians, and other educators. These are useful to parents. However, when parents talk to parents, there is greater receptivity. Parents who have been involved in the reading activities are in an even better position to share their experiences. The following collection of ideas and advice from parents and teachers could be presented in a simple newsletter. The items are written specifically for parents, and they can help in preventing and correcting reading difficulties.

1. Use Problems as Learning Experiences

The home is the first place where children can obtain a sense of warmth and security where they can express their feelings and gain self-confidence. Maintaining that kind of an atmosphere helps children grow into secure human beings. It's a good idea to give special attention to helping your children handle problems and obstacles before and as they occur. Think up problem situations and ask your child what he or she would do. Listen to and talk with your child. Use every problem as a learning experience. Discuss different ways of handling the same problem.

2. Reading in the Living Environment

Sometimes this concept is called "reading in the kitchen." It means encouraging your children to read directions on food cartons and in recipes. Such items as cereal boxes and milk cartons can also be used as reading lessons. Or you can label furniture and have your child read the labels. Simple word games are another part of this concept. There is both power and inspiration in reading familiar objects in your own environment.

3. Talk to Develop Language Facility

There is no better way to develop language than through discussion and dialogue. Talking begets talking. When you speak in complete sentences and discuss topics of interest it can help your children develop language facility. The more children use language, the greater their ability to communicate. One of the memorable childhood joys is conversing with parents. Plan time for the family to talk. Set aside at least one evening a week for this joyful activity.

4. Find Reading Role-Models

Homes where reading is a natural part of the family activities help instill in children the idea that reading is a part of living. Research shows that children from families who read tend to have less difficulty with reading. Children do what their parents do. The actual reading material is not as important as the reading act itself. For example, many families read the newspaper, the Bible, manuals related to their occupations, letters, and magazines.

5. Read to Your Child

The importance of reading to your young child cannot be stressed too much or too intensely. Perhaps more than any other single activity, reading to your children affects their interest in reading. The old bedtime stories remain a good learning tool for teaching and inspiring.

6. Relating to Teachers

A working relationship with the classroom teacher is critical to understanding and assisting children with reading difficulties. Even for children who have no special problem, teachers can aid parents in enriching and expanding reading interests. Volunteering in the classroom is another way to provide support. Establish a relationship with the teachers and let them know of your interest, concern, and desire to help. Generously share observations of your child's interests or problems with the teacher.

7. Knowing Your Child's Problem

Reading difficulties are many and vared. Parents should find out about their child's specific deficiency. Here again, teachers can provide the specifics and suggest ways of assisting. Parents themselves, through observation of children's reading, can determine some of the problems. Discussing these observations with your child's teacher can prevent more compliated difficulties.

8. Give Positive Reinforcement

Most people react to praise, encouragement, and positiveness. "Stroking," as it is commonly called, is a simple but powerful weapon which helps individuals feel and act responsively. Children are no different from adults. They, too, respond to stroking. When your youngster has difficulty with reading, he or she needs a great deal of encouragement. Failure is devastating to the human personality. Therefore, as a parent, you can help tremendously by positively reinforcing the areas of need and praising progress. Keep your criticism at a minimum.

9. Supervise Homework

Parents have traditionally assumed the responsibility for homework supervision. In an age when there are other distractions such as television, radio, stereo, club meetings, and music lessons, your children need more than ever to set aside quiet time for study. When you as parents monitor their assignments, the results are improved student performance. This is particularly true in the area of reading. It is a fact that the more one reads, the better one reads.

10. Attend Parent Education Classes

In most communities, adult education and parent education classes are available. These classes can be helpful in skill development and staff improvement. The establishment of parent education classes to deal with reading and helping children with reading deficiencies is a growing area in adult education. Enroll, if possible. If these are not available, use your child's teacher as a resource.

11. Create a Home Learning Environment

—Make your home emotionally comfortable for children. Your child should feel free to express his or her joys and sorrows. Being able to discuss a problem, feeling accepted and secure, knowing parents will listen to his or her ideas and opinions—all are part of positive family relationships. These feelings nurture children's attitudes and enhance their readiness to pursue reading.

—Provide a place, even a corner, for your child to be alone to think, read, and pursue his or her own interests.

—Establish with your child a budget, ever so modest, for purchasing inexpensive paperback books. A home library is an important ingredient in stimulating children to read. However, if this is not possible, the public library is available.

—Regular use of the public library is an excellent way to increase reading, and it also makes books available at no cost.

—Leave magazines and newspapers for your children to read. In fact, ask them leading questions so there will be a purpose for reading.

12. Pursue Family Hobbies

Pursuing family hobbies and projects can involve your child in learning. These need not be complex or expensive. They might include planting a garden, collecting coins or other less expensive items, building toys or furniture, or caring for pets. Many other practical projects could be started. These activities offer opportunities for children to be actively involved and will necessitate some reading. Plan time for the family to talk. With the hectic schedules of parents and children, it is sometimes difficult to have a relaxed conversation. The family could set aside one evening a week for the entire group to discuss anything that surfaces.

13. Display Your Child's Work

Find some way to display your child's schoolwork someplace in the house. Here again, this need not be fancy, but children are proud of their accomplishments, and displaying them on the mantle, refrigerator, or on a family bulletin board can build a sense of pride and self-esteem. Feelings of appreciation and self-confidence are important in promoting reading progress.

14. Monitor TV Programs

Guide the television viewing in such a way that your children are not dominated by TV. Limiting the amount of time for watching is crucial (to an hour a day). Monitoring the types of programs your children watch is important, too. Children tend to use TV as a substitute for reading. There are many less passive activities that can stretch the mind and foster reading development.

MORE SUGGESTIONS FOR HELPING CHILDREN WITH READING

The following suggestions can also be shared with parents and can help get them involved in assisting the child at home as well as in establishing a relationship with the teacher at school.

—Releate reading to practical realities. For example, labeling every piece of furniture in your child's room is a good start on words and their meaning.
—Allow your child to read and work at his or her own pace. It is tempting to push, and it is easy to become impatient; but if children are permitted to read frequently and at a speed that is comfortable for them, their progress will be evident.

15. Build on What Your Child Knows

Encourage your child to talk and read about those things that are of interest. You can increase vocabulary by starting with words that the child knows.

16. Teach for Understanding

As you teach the ABCs, be sure that your child understands the letter he or she is reciting. The connection between what is said and read is important for later word and sentence development.

17. Teach to Ability

Gain an understanding of your child' ability and don't try

to get him or her to be a genius if he or she is not. Steady progress is the key, not great leaps.

18. Plan Short Sessions

Different children have varying interest spans. Plan when your child is not tired so that he or she does not begin to dread the reading activities.

19. Use Your Child's Interests and Strengths

In assisting your child, begin with topics of interest to him or her. Children are much more likely to progress if they are interested in the subject. Also, you know the child's strengths, so identify his or her strong characteristics and use them in your sessions. If he or she is good at writing, then have him or her write something to read. If your child speaks well, offer poetry and rhymes. Whatever the strengths, capitalize on them in the reading endeavors.

READING-RELATED MATERIALS FOR PARENTS

Following is a brief but important list of publications for use by parents who desire to explore further in the area of reading.
1. Ervin, Jane. *Your Child Can Read and You Can Help (A Book for Parents)*. Garden City, N.Y.: Doubleday & Co., Inc., 1979.

2. Rosner, Jerome. *Helping Children Overcome Learning Difficulties.* New York, N.Y.: Walker & Co., 1975.
3. Smith, Carl B., and Fay, Leo C. *Getting People to Read.* New York, N.Y.: Dell Publishing Co., 1973.
4. U.S. Department of Health Education and Welfare. *Tutor's Resource Handbook.* Department of Health Education and Welfare, No. (OE) 74-00101, Washington, D.C., 1974.

8
A SUMMARY OF READING APPROACHES AND METHODS

It is characteristic of the public in general and parents in particular to inquire as to which method of teaching reading works best. The question is posed as if the solution is in the method.

Several studies, as well as teachers' practical experiences, have concurred with the finding that reading approaches are important, but reading approaches alone do not make the significant difference in reading achievement. Nonetheless, most agree that it is critical for classroom teachers to understand the variety of reading approaches and methods of instruction that can best relate to individual children's interests, needs, and learning styles. Frequently, a child may respond to one specific method and not to another. Therefore, having knowledge and understanding of the multiple methods of reading will enable the teacher to make a better match between the child and the methodology. Teachers who understand these methods and bring to reading their own techniques, styles, and understandings can have significant impact on the ultimate achievement of children. In most cases, teachers use several approaches or methods within one classroom. The literature refers to such a variety of approaches as *eclectic*. This simply means that the good teachers provide alternatives to children of varying levels development and learning style.

The specific approaches described briefly in this chapter include: basal reader approach, language experience approach, individualized reading, and diagnostic-prescriptive approach. These descriptions offer basic knowledge that teachers should possess about reading approaches, and which may serve to help parents in their understanding of what goes on in the classroom.

BASAL READER APPROACH

This approach to developmental reading instruction utilizes a graded series of reading books and related materials. Usually, a basal reader approach begins with the development of a sight vocabulary, features controlled vocabulary, and teaches critical reading skills with major emphasis on comprehension and a secondary emphasis on word recognition techniques.

Most basal reading programs suggest that teachers interact with small groups to reinforce the reading process. In recent years, reading instruction has focused on diagnosing and assessing children's needs, and meeting those needs in various ways. On this basis, the basal reader approach guides teachers in motivating children to discuss new words and explore concepts, ideas, and meanings. The instructional format involves silent reading, oral reading and discussion, skill introduction or review, and reinforcement activities to be done either with teacher direction or independently. Usually available are a variety of supplementary materials that relate to individual children's needs. Most basal reading programs provide a management system to assure skill mastery.

Basal reading series are identified by the name of the particular publisher. Rarely do titles specify the basic methodology, and rarely are those methodologies presented in pure form.

Individual basal reading programs are distinguished by their methodology as well as their instructional progression and pacing. The classical, research-supported methods currently in use are linguistics and phonics.

• Linguistic Methods

Linguistic methods place strong emphasis on structural elements in language, and their role in decoding. Children learn how to relate speech units and patterns to their printed symbols. Further, this method draws on the structure of the English language as children are alerted to the order and grouping of word patterns, word arrangements in sentences, punctuation marks, and aspects of grammar as clues to meaning.

In combination, the skills presented through this method provide a unique approach to aspects of comprehension as well as word recognition.

• Phonics Method

Phonics refers to a method of recognizing an unfamiliar word. Unlike a linguistic method which directly impacts decoding and comprehension, phonics has direct impact just on decoding, and is a word-recognition method considered highly effective for beginning reading. Comprehension still remains a primary focus in this type of basal series, but uses more conventional techniques.

Most basal reading programs involve some phonics in that they make the child very aware of sound-symbol associations, and teach word analysis techniques to be applied independently at a later time.

First children learn one sound for one printed symbol, and soon build words by blending together a series of sound-symbol relationships. In a matter of a few weeks, children learn to tackle multiple sounds for one symbol, and more complex word elements. The assumption is that children who build consistent word recognition technique can read more material with greater confidence, and sooner, which is a built-in source of motivation.

LANGUAGE EXPERIENCE

Language experience approach to reading has as its major focus the use of childrens' own language and experiences as the basis for the program of reading instruction. The premise behind this approach is that children will be more interested in reading if what they read relates to their own experiences and language. Therefore, oral language is very much a part of this approach and children are urged to think about their experiences, to express their ideas and thoughts, and to read and review these experiences in written form. Teachers use eclectic methods for teaching word recognition techniques and comprehension skills. Most of the reading material in the language experience approach is produced by the children themselves. The program in this approach involves reading as an integral part of other language arts. Unlike other reading approaches, the vocabulary is not controlled; however, there are an expansive number of words that are used as children become comfortable in expressing their experiences and ideas. As the child progresses, a variety of children's books are used to enhance the children's experiences.

INDIVIDUALIZED READING

Individualized reading usually assumes that a basal reading approach or language experience approach has been used to teach beginning reading. Individualized reading is a method of instruction that stresses the need to diagnose the needs and learning style of each child and to allow each child to select his or her reading materials from a wide variety of materials available. Fundamental to the individualized reading is the fact that children will read not only different materials but at different rates. Teachers listen to the individual children read during scheduled conferences with them. The teacher reviews at that time the child's progress in word attack and comprehension. Student profiles or records are kept on each child in the individualized reading program. It is important that each child be kept aware of the progress being made and problem areas. Children are encourage to focus on their deficiencies. Some individualized reading programs involve small group instruction for like skills among several children. However, the major focus is on the individual and the individual's reading approach. There is no prescribed set of books, as library books and teacher or student collected reading materials are used.

DIAGNOSTIC-PRESCRIPTIVE INSTRUCTION

The diagnostic-prescriptive reading approach requires an analysis of the student's reading deficiencies and for these deficiencies to be recorded on a chart or profile. Diagnostic tests (commercial or teacher-developed) are used. Each child in the class then has a prescription related to his or her reading deficiencies. As the child masters certain prescriptions, these are checked off and indicated as progress. In the diagnostic-prescriptive aproach, there tends to be more emphasis on mastering specific skills than on practicing them in combination. However, once there is a level of skill proficiency, the focus turns to using skills in combination. Very often programmed instruction is used as one of the major methods of prescribing for needs. Similar to the individualized approach, the teacher forms small groups to assist with problem areas. Reinforcement for progress is a definite part of the diagnostic-prescriptive approach.

CONCLUSION

Since our classrooms are composed of a wide variety of individual children with learning needs and interests, it is essential for the teacher to recognize that no single method of reading instruction is so superior to another than the method alone can determine the reading progress of the students. It is true, however, that teachers who are familiar with a variety of approaches and comfortable using them can in fact improve the reading achievement of students significantly. Therefore, a composite of methods can and have produced the best results. Frequently, in fact too frequently, emphasis on reading is placed on reading deficiencies. We would urge that teachers look at both the reading deficiencies and the strengths of students as we build programs that allow children to learn the skills of reading while enjoying and comprehending what they read.

ADMINISTRATIVE LEADERSHIP AND SUPPORT

9
ENSURING SUCCESSFUL READING PROGRAMS

A comprehensive look at successful reading programs uncovers significant commonalities. Information about these common ingredients can be used by administrators, teachers, and parents in planning, modifying, or assessing programs of reading to ensure success. The common factors can be divided into two broad categories: external (factors which support the overall school reading program) and internal (factors within the classroom reading programs itself).

EXTERNAL FACTORS FOR SUCCESSFUL READING PROGRAMS

On the face of it, external factors may appear to have little to do with successful reading programs. Yet careful scrutiny indicates that they have a tremendous impact on reading. In the main, they establish a climate for quality education. Often a classroom reading program may be well designed, but the outside factors are such that there is insufficient support for total implementation.

Reading needs to be reinforced by any number of variables within a district and a school. Certain external factors, including a high priority for reading throughout the curriculum, effective leadership, systematic planning, and a skilled staff, need to be present to provide a supportive setting and atmosphere in which the intructional program can flourish. Therefore, if attention is paid to these external factors, which are discussed in the following sections, initiating and implementing reading activities is simplified.

Reading as a Priority

Reading, if it is to permeate the school district and the community, needs the commitment of the school board and the superintendent. For successful programs support should be provided from the highest levels, and attention to reading should be continuous. The attention to reading by officials should include major aspects of the program parameters—for instance, methods and materials, competencies and costs, planning and productivity, staffing and evaluation. The school district's staff should express their priorities in terms of words and deeds. When goals, objectives, and expectations are high, and assistance is provided to schools in meeting them, the changes of success are maximal. In other words, a vast amount of support given to personnel and parents is critical in both the formal and informal reading activities.

In considering reading as a priority, pertinent questions should be raised regarding time, money, and quality. For example—

- —How much time is spent on reading and reading support activities in the district, the school, the classroom, and the home?
- —What is the level of financial resources expended on the total reading effort, such as for people, books and aids, motivational ideas, and creative activities?
- —Does the quality of the program assure that most students will improve?
- —How is the program planned, monitored, and serviced in order to maintain momentum and direction?
- —What kind of accountability and evaluation systems are built into the program design?

Appropriate responses to these queries can determine priority status in school districts and communities. Perhaps the greatest influence in setting reading priority is in the unleashing of the "people potential" to focus on reading.

In the normal course of events, reading programs tend to become an adjunct to the existing activities and are likely to be phased out as special funds diminish. Conversely, as districts adopt reading as a priority, the likelihood of sustained, systematic changes is maximized. The arm of priority should reach from the superintendent's office to the classroom.

Effective Leadership

Every recent study, from those conducted by the Council on Basic Education to those conducted by the Educational Testing Service, found the overridingly important ingredient in a school program to be viable leadership. Just as forceful leadership by the superintendent sets the tone for the school district, strong school management and leadership ability in the principal is a critical variable in program implementation and ultimate effectiveness. Interestingly, administrative style is less important than the ability to foster a climate for positive, constructive activities.

While the principal is not expected to be a reading expert, he or she should know about reading and be able to facilitate and monitor. Further, the principal should be able to assess teachers' effectiveness in teaching and provide the opportunity for professional growth and development.

It is singularly important that the administrator understands how to involve people (teachers, parents, and others) in programs, from planning to evaluation. It is also the leader who articulates the expectations, maintains standards of staff performance, communicates to the broader community the reading priority, and ascertains emphasis on reading in the relevant activities.

Systematic Program Planning

The district and school leadership decide when, who, and how systematic program planning is to evolve in order to capitalize on the expertise and interests of the staff and community representatives. The degree to which beneficiaries participate in the planning of the program relates significantly to the chances for success in implementation. If students are to be served, they should have some input in the program. Parents also should be actively involved in planning. Since teachers are key personnel, they should be participants in program design and planning. Related personnel, such as specialists, consultants, aides, and tutors, can contribute positively to program formulation.

It is a proven fact that the more involved people are in the formative stages of a program, the greater the chances of success. Indeed, an overriding aspect of successful reading programs is the involvement of an array of persons in the planning process.

A district profile of reading should be established based on a thorough needs assessment. Then goals and objectives can be set and alternative strategies for implementation established. Strengths and weaknesses should be weighed. Finally, personnel and parents should be asked to assume responsibility and the evaluation designed. Planning systematically is a vital step in the pursuit of excellence.

Staff Selection

Education is a people business. One of the most important decisions to be made by administration in setting up a reading program is the screening and selection of personnel. The necessity for competent staff cannot be overemphasized. In any program, staff represents an extension of the management. Qualities critical to educational performance include—

Dedication and professionalism
Expertise in teaching reading

Positive human relations skills in handling students with less than satisfactory achievement
Cooperation among team members
Support personnel such as librarians, counselors, psychologists, and teacher aides should also possess these qualities and skills.

The groups that work with students need a large portion of confidence, commitment, and competence. For a successful program, enormous emphasis should be placed on the adequacy of the personnel; and this single fact can represent the difference between an average and a good program.

Comprehensive Education

Reading is not an isolated subject. It can be enhanced by being an integral part of a multifaceted education program designed to meet the multiple needs and interests of students. As districts pursue basic skills—particularly reading—it seems clear that reading can be learned in a variety of settings and in different courses. Reading can indeed be effectively taught and learned in social studies, science, mathematics, and music, as well as other courses. The impetus for reading can also be derived from sources other than reading classes or reading periods. The content of a subject, a course, or an activity often ignites a spark, thereby increasing interest and skill development. Because most subjects and courses require the use of reading, in this context reading should be the prerogative of every teacher, just as comprehensive education should be the goal of the school. When education is all-encompassing, the opportunity for progress is enhanced, and the chances for addressing various intellects and interests are increased. Reading programs should definitely depend upon the entire school curriculum. Each teacher should be cognizant of the reading needs of students and build reading instructions into the fabric of every course.

Reading improvement also depends on support services. Having available medical, psychological, dental, and other vital services means problematic barriers are removed.

INTERNAL FACTORS FOR SUCCESSFUL READING PROGRAMS

We know students learned to read in some programs. In fact they can make impressive gains in reading performance. Why? What are the ingredients within reading programs which help children learn to read? Some common factors which present themselves as forceful internal aspects of effective reading endeavors are described in the following sections.

Reading Strategies and Methods

Well-planned lessons and organized followups based on needs of students are important aspects of effective reading programs. Some type of diagnostic measurement of students is essential in reading programs. Such diagnosis relates to both the weaknesses and the strengths of students. The diagnostic instruments may range from informal teacher-developed instruments to formal standardized tests. In any case, information regarding a student's deficiency should be immediately available so as to guide the teacher in the instructional process. However, we should also remember that most teachers feel recordkeeping should not be excessive, classes should not be too large, and assistance should be available for testing.

For the most part, programs that are successful are predicated on a set of standards which include clear goals and objectives. Curriculum guides should stipulate activities to meet these standards.

Teachers tend to follow their reading diagnosis with reinforcements or prescriptions. To the extent feasible, students should be made aware of their problems and progress on an immediate basis. Emphasis should be on individual reading needs of students.

There is no one reading method which is more effective than another. A variety of methods is used in most reading programs. However, the approaches to reading should be discrete and teachers should be intensely aware of the methodologies. Definite reading approaches with complementary materials can be enormously helpful. Some of the more frequently used methods in reading programs are individualized instruction, language experience, programmed instruction, phonetic reading, and diagnostic-prescriptive approaches.

Emphasis should be placed on word recognition, comprehension, vocabulary, and inferences. Both oral and written communications are significant aspects of reading lessons.

Generally, reading programs are either corrective or remedial and, of course, aimed at improving the skills of individuals who are underachieving. Developmental reading should be used as students progress. Good programs should stress that students progress at their own rates and include profiles and charts to follow the students' progress. Due to students short attention spans, activities should change fairly quickly.

Plans to motivate and stimulate interest in reading should

be built into the fabric of reading programs. Discovering individual interests should be emphasized almost as much as diagnosing deficiencies. The thought here is to guarantee student stimulation. Rewards and incentives (Nonmonetary) can also be used. As was said earlier, such reinforcement is a powerful motivational tool and significantly enhances programs.

Independent reading in the form of "free time" should be of primary concern, for students need time to explore and enjoy reading on their own. They can also benefit from reading privately. Closely related is the freedom to choose books, magazines, and other reading materials. Self-selection seems to be quite popular both with students and teachers. In a sense, it represents having some control over one's destiny or exercising a choice.

The teaching process can be enhanced by the use of equipment such as tape recorders, filmstrip projectors, and records. Although supplementary, the aids are important to the lesson. They can provide valuable opportunities for students to speak, listen, and evaluate their own reading.

Reading programs should be teacher-directed but with much opportunity for individual options. Reading, however, should not be left to chance. To be effective, lessons need to be goal-centered and directed at achieving specific objectives. They need to be both challenging and enjoyable.

Relevant Books and Materials

Books and other reading materials support the reading program. They are not the program. Far too often textbooks become the reading program. For successful programs, teacher-developed and commercial materials should be carefully selected to coincide with the needs of the students and the reading methods. Both diagnostic and prescriptive reading materials are used widely. Within a given classroom, several sets of books, as well as library books, should be available. Reading teachers may prepare their own materials especially, reading games, flash cards, and creative writing which can help in motivational and skill building areas.

As a general rule, the commercial materials are sequential as well as developmental. After the initial lesson, students should have access to learning centers, listening posts, tape recorders, and library books and games. The classrooms should also provide inexpensive paperback books, magazines, and newspapers. Students should be urged to bring from home relevant reading materials. Much use can be made of students' writings as valuable reading materials: stories, essays, and poems all contribute to reading.

The entire program staff should be familiar with reading methods and diverse materials.

Reading is a rich and enriching activity. Students should be challenged to discover, explore, seek information, and obtain answers. The selection of cogent materials can help individual students in these endeavors, thereby resulting in improved reading performance.

Stimulating Classroom Climate

The atmosphere in a classroom can be a powerful force in stimulating students to read—or not to read. For successful programs, classroom climates should be aesthetic without being expensive, open without being chaotic, inviting without being overbearing. Such an atmosphere generates warmth and excitement and provides a place where students, worn from failure and fatigue, can find acceptance and some success.

Teachers may find it necessary to use concrete objects and real life experiences, and to change displays and exhibits frequently. In the process, they should involve students, aides, tutors, and parents. Perhaps the most positive attraction in a classroom is the teacher's own attitude toward the students. Special effort should be made to seek out and to understand not only a student's reading difficulties but his or her cultural milieu as well. With the diversity represented in many classrooms, teachers should expend large amounts of time and energy trying to make each youngster feel worthwhile. Developing and nurturing self-concepts and self-confidence pays rewarding dividends as classroom climates evolve. Indeed, a positive environment opens new doors of opportunity and turns students toward reading.

Parental Involvement and Support

As indicated in Chapter 6, students show improvement in reading when parents are involved in planning programs and reinforcing reading lessons.

Parents usually have a great deal of helpful information about their children. This information can be useful in analyzing the needs and strengths of students. Close collaboration between parents and teachers is an important ingredient in successful programs.

In an exchange of salient data, parents become aware of ways to help their youngsters, to reinforce lessons. Concurrently, teachers learn much from parents.

Parent-teacher reading conferences or meetings in which

the student profile forms the basis of discussion can be mutually beneficial. Combining recognition of progress and assistance for weaknesses should form the core of aid from both teachers and parents. Children frequently improve in direct proportion to the levels and intensity of support from their parents.

For successful projects, parental participation should be solicited from the inception of the program. Parents then feel the program is theirs, as they have shared in the planning, implementation, and evaluation.

A major factor in successful programs is the development of the range of communication skills on the part of parents. These skills can be used in assisting their children, not only with reading related homework but also with special lessons at home.

Two of the byproducts of parent involvement are increased adult interest in their own education and expanded reading habits. Both of these can benefit the students as well as the parents.

Staff Competencies and Expectations

The key ingredient in successful programs is the staff. The staff team forms the human variable which contributes more than anything else to reading effectiveness. All members of the education team—administrator, specialist, teacher, tutor, aide, volunteer—are critical, but the central responsibility for teaching rests with the teacher. Indeed, the expertise and responsibility of teachers are awesome. The knowledge of the teacher in the pedagogy of reading, the skill in instructing, the high expectation of students, the expertise in motivating and sustaining interest are all highly contributory factors to improved reading performance. Staff competencies in these areas should be undergirded by an abiding commitment to youth. In those situations in which reading specialists assume primary responsibility for remedial reading, it still remains the classroom teacher's role to provide reading instruction and reinforcement of the special lessons and to work closely with the specialist. In other words, there is no substitute for the classroom teacher.

In today's education complexities, the role of the teacher is broadened considerably to include areas such as supervision of aides, volunteers, tutors, assistants; human relations; communications with diverse cultural and socioeconomic groups; and community relations involving parents and citizen representatives. The implications for staff selection criteria and inservice training are obvious. Staff members need continual revitalization and replenishment as they tackle the enormous tasks required in the instructional program. Participation is a very important support activity.

Staff Involvement and Development

Closely related to personnel selection are the involvement and professional growth opportunities available to staff. Student performance can be richly enhanced when staff is involved in designed the program. Just as parent participation contributes to programs, so staff involvement adds a vital dimension to program effectiveness. When the implementors are on the planning team, there is a deeper sense of commitment to the concepts and methodologies. The result, of course, is better student achievement. When teachers have the opportunity to observe, interact, and share innovative practices, they are able to contribute highly to the success of reading projects.

Staff development, to be meaningful, and effective, should address individual as well as group needs, desires, and interests. In addition to the chance for professional growth in the teaching of reading, teachers and other personnel should be involved in the ongoing coordination and operation of the program. Inservice education for and with the teaching support staff should be a part of the training efforts. Teamwork is significant to program success.

Teachers often need assistance in the following areas:

Diagnostic/prescriptive teaching. This area is a frequently required aspect in federal and state programs with limited teacher preparation.

Motivation. The techniques for turning students on and maintaining a level of interest and enthusiasm are vital for teachers. In most instances, some attention should be given to students from diverse economic and cultural backgrounds.

Individualizing instruction. Teachers may need help with how to make it happen in a class of thirty-five students who are economically and ethnically diverse.

Working with parents. An understanding of how to involve parents in reinforcing reading during the many hours a youngster is away from school may be another need.

Selecting materials. With the enormous amount of commercialized materials on the market, teachers are frequently unclear as to the merit of available reading matter. Teachers need to know about criteria for selecting the reading materials which most effectively meet individual and group needs in terms of program goals and objectives.

Creating a reading climate. The entire school district can foster a positive environment for reading improvement. Reading should be stimulated, recognized, and rewarded. Motivation is an intrinsic key to reading, and environment plays a vital role. A district can ill afford *not* to offer a variety of methods to stimulate students to read.

A positive method of initiating staff development plans is to have teachers assess their own skills and needs. Seeking assistance to strengthen particular areas can become a more meaningful process when it is based on self-assessment. The form shown on pages 124–125 may be used by teachers to ascertain for themselves those areas in which they want and need to improve their skills.

TEACHER AND PARAPROFESSIONAL SKILLS ASSESSMENT FORM

	VERY GOOD	GOOD	NEEDS IMPROVEMENT	CAN OBTAIN HELP FROM
A. STANDARDS AND EXPECTATIONS • Has high but realistic standards for progress for each child • Communicates these expectations to each student • Creates an atmosphere in which each student can improve				
B. MOTIVATING STUDENTS • Develops and maintains children's interest in reading • Learns as much as possible about each student's interests • Establishes an example by using his or her own reading skills • Makes available a variety of reading materials • Helps each child to feel important and to let each student know he or she is expected to read				
C. ORGANIZATION FOR READING • Plans for adequate time for all aspects of reading program • Plans instructional activities around a comprehensive sequential reading program				
D. DIAGNOSING READING DIFFICULTIES • Analyzes each student's needs for assistance in reading program • Selects and uses appropriate diagnostic instruments • Establishes a student profile for each student				

TEACHER AND PARAPROFESSIONAL SKILLS ASSESSMENT FORM

	VERY GOOD	GOOD	NEEDS IMPROVEMENT	CAN OBTAIN HELP FROM
E. PRESCRIBING FOR STUDENT'S READING NEEDS • Understands and uses alternative reading approaches • Uses appropriate reading materials to meet specific instruction needs • Is able to teach the skills necessary for the individual student • Provides individual assistance to students with special needs • Uses evaluative instruments to test individual objectives • Has the problems and progress charted in student profile				
F. INVOLVES PARENTS • Communicates the reading problems with students' parents • Offers specific suggestions as to how parents can help child • Assigns reading related to homework regularly • Communicates progress to parent and student				

This chart was adapted and modified from Right to Read Handbook, U.S. Government Printing Office, 1974, Washington, D.C.

Reading Success — Districtwide Ingredients

At the risk of sounding too prescriptive we offer the following set of questions which may serve as a guide in either planning or assessing reading programs.

Does the program have—

- Well-defined measureable objectives for the district, the school, and the child?
- Approaches and methods based on theory and understood by teachers?
- Communication skills that help students to think, speak, write, and listen?
- Techniques and methods of diagnosing, prescribing, and informing students of their levels of achievement?
- Broad, sequentially ordered components in word recognition, comprehension, and vocabulary?
- Provisions for indepth educational and noneducational diagnosis of strengths?
- Curriculum relevant to the cultural, ethnic, and economic diversity in the classroom?
- Learning expectations and standards for each level and guides as to learning capabilities?
- Materials to which students from diverse backgrounds can relate?
- Provisions for success and progress for students from varying achievement levels?
- Techniques for ensuring continuity of methods and materials for individuals and groups?
- A method for ongoing documentation and assessment of individual student performances?

—Provisions for embracing all subjects, such as social science, math, and science? In other words, are we stressing learning to read and reading to learn?

Cycle of Program Development

Successful programs should be systematic cycles of program development. Some phases may need to be stressed more than others, depending upon the local situation. An orderly process should include the following:

Assessment. As much as possible should be learned about the existing reading programs, methods used, varying materials, and amounts of time.

Development. The most effective staff and citizens should be utilized to determine standards and guides, objectives, activities, reading methods. Criteria for textbooks should be set and a program plan developed.

Implementation. A team should operate in sequential steps.

Evaluation. The evaluation and assessment design should be set up at the beginning of the program. Evaluation goes hand in hand with needs assessment, and programs should have periodic check points. Formal and informal instruments should be used.

Feedback and modification. The staff should have a system for determining and disseminating those components and processes which work well under given circumstances. An information feedback procedure helps staff instruct, coordinate, and plan more effectively.

Accountability system. Each member of the reading team should have a well-defined role and set of objectives with a timeline. Being responsible for the accomplishment of those objectives is necessary if the program is to meet its goals and purpose.

CONCLUSION

Improving the quality of reading calls for defined roles and definitive programs. The administrator, reading specialist, coordinator, psychologist, teacher, librarian, aides, and parents should know what is expected. Since some 90 percent of all reading instruction occurs within the classroom, it is imperative that educators demystify the reading process and clearly delineate what a school's reading program encompasses.

Reading success cannot be left to chance. It necessitates planning, development, implementation, and evaluation as well as ongoing monitoring and modification. In other words, reading programs which are effective are in the process of continual renewal.

Placing priority on reading and on developing and maintaining viable programs presents a significant challenge. It means perhaps resructuring priorities, eliminating some activities, and making painful decisions. While it is not an easy task, it is an exciting opportunity to serve as an agent for reading. In *The Prince* Machiavelli wrote, "There is nothing more difficult to carry out, more hazardous to conduct, or more uncertain as to its success, than to initiate a new order of things." Reading improvement often requires a new order of things.

10
SCHOOLWIDE READING ASSESSMENT

Effective reading starts with the individual child. However, for the majority of students to be literate, reading must be a priority. The individual, the group, the class, and the school should be exposed to the most stimulating reading instruction programs during the first year of school.

How do we improve reading within the total school? We all know it is not by chance. Reading assessment is a logical place to begin. This chapter includes an amalgamation of assessment instruments designed to analyze reading programs on a schoolwide basis. Of course, assessment is just the first step; planning, followed by staff development and implementation, is the logical sequence.

As the school team or committee initiates its assessment and planning process, goals and objectives are necessary as a guide and should be reviewed in terms of the entire school.

SOME GOALS AND OBJECTIVES FOR A READING PROGRAM

1. Student will comprehend written materials.

Student will develop a variety of comprehension strategies.
- —Identifies word meaning
- —Pinpoints and enumerates main ideas and supporting details directly stated and implied
  Identifies relationships, directly stated and implied
- —Follows written directions accurately
- —Uses writing style to interpret writer's intent
- —Identifies writing style and literary techniques
- —Evaluates written materials critically.

Student will develop a variety of word attack skills and will use those particular skills that most efficiently permit him or her to unlock unknown words.
- —Uses context clues, structural analysis, and phonics clues in addition to the dictionary to unlock unknown words.

Student will demonstrate flexibility in rate of reading.
- —Selects speed and techniques in terms of purpose for reading
- —Selects reading techniques in terms of difficulty of reading task
- —Reads as rapidly as difficulty level of material will permit.

Student will use work-study skills in obtaining specific information in reading.
- —Uses reference aids in books to locate specific sources of information
- —Uses library reference skills to locate specific sources of information
- —Uses encyclopedias, source books, and specialized reference works to obtain specific information
- —Takes notes, and outlines and summarizes materials that are read
- —Develops a plan of study
- —Locates and interprets specific information from maps, tables, graphs, and other pictorial materials.

Student will develop the special reading skills related to the various subject areas in which he or she reads.
- —Develops the technical vocabulary of each subject area
- —Develops the concept background of each subject area that is needed for understanding what is read
- —Uses strategies that are most appropriate for reading material in a particular subject area
- —Uses any special reading techniques that are a part of a particular subject area
- —Interprets symbols and abbreviations correctly when they are a part of a subject area.

2. Student will consider all aspects of reading aloud

Understands when it is appropriate to read aloud
- —Reads aloud to inform others
- —Reads aloud to enjoy the rhythm of poetry
- —Reads aloud to improve skills in oral reading.

Shows Accurate pronunciation and enunciation
- —Pronounces words accurately in oral reading
- —Enunciates word endings in a natural speaking voice.

Uses voice and body to interpret what is being read.
- —Uses rate, pitch, tone, and quality to interpret writer's intent
- —Phrases sentences appropriately in oral reading
- —Maintains occasional eye contact with audience during oral reading
- —Sits or stands in comfortable position while reading orally.

3. Student will react to and understand what he or she reads.

Student will develop permanent interests in reading.
- —Develops a variety of interests that may be used to motivate reading
- —Seeks books and other reading materials that are related to his or her interests
- —Reads a variety of types of reading matter.

Student will develop literary tastes and appreciations.
- —Identifies elements of style and form
- —Identifies story problem and solution
- —Identifies traits and motives of characters
- —Judges the relative merit of several pieces of literature
- —Selects reading materials of good quality.

FLOW CHART FOR READING PROGRAM ASSESSMENT AND PLAN

```
┌─────────────────────────┐
│        Identify         │
│   Student Population    │
└─────────────────────────┘
             ▼
┌─────────────────────────┐
│     Assess Existing     │
│     Reading Program     │
└─────────────────────────┘
             ▼
┌─────────────────────────┐
│  Identify New Objectives│
└─────────────────────────┘
             ▼
┌─────────────────────────┐
│    Review Successful    │
│    Reading Programs     │
└─────────────────────────┘
             ▼
┌─────────────────────────┐
│      Plan New or        │
│    Modified Program     │
└─────────────────────────┘
             ▼
┌─────────────────────────┐
│    Identify Reading     │
│  Approaches and Methods │
└─────────────────────────┘
             ▼
┌─────────────────────────┐
│ Select Appropriate Materials │
└─────────────────────────┘
             ▼
┌─────────────────────────┐
│   Identify Staff Needs  │
└─────────────────────────┘
             ▼
┌─────────────────────────┐
│       Plan Parent       │
│   Involvement Program   │
└─────────────────────────┘
             ▼
┌─────────────────────────┐
│  Plan Staff Development │
└─────────────────────────┘
             ▼
┌─────────────────────────┐
│   Develop Evaluation    │
│         Design          │
└─────────────────────────┘
```

BASIC SCHOOL DATA

(A) Name of School _____

(B) Grade or Level

(C) Enrollment by Grade or Level

(D) Committee (Name of Members):

Reading Specialist _____

District Office Administrator _____

Parents _____

Others _____

Principal _____

Teachers _____

Librarian _____

Teacher Aides _____

Student Teachers _____

ADDITIONAL DATA

(E) Community Represented: _____ Inner City _____ City
_____ Suburban _____ Rural

(F) Ethnic/Racial Distribution:
_____% Native American _____% Asian _____% Black
_____% Hispanics _____% White _____% Other

(G) On A.F.D.C. _____%, or Other Indices of Socioeconomic Level _____%

(H) Mobility (Last Three Years): _____% Students _____% Teachers

Note: After a committee or team is formed, the basic information provided by this form about the school can give everyone a clear knowledge of the population to be served.

READING PROGRAM ASSESSMENT CHART

PROGRAM ELEMENTS: Student Performance, Program Organization, Resources—Staff & Materials

GRADE OR LEVEL   RANKED PRIORITY

A. STUDENT PERFORMANCE   Record months or below norm:
    Standardized Tests
    Word Recognition
    Vocabulary
    Reading Comprehension
    Spelling
    Word Usage
    Study Skills
    Verbal Skills
    Sentence

B. OTHER MEASURES   Answer yes or no and rate 1, 2, 3, 4, or 5
    Are Criterion-Referenced tests given to students?
    Are Informal Reading Inventories given to students?
    Is an Attitude Toward Reading Survey given?
    Is a Reading Interest Inventory given?

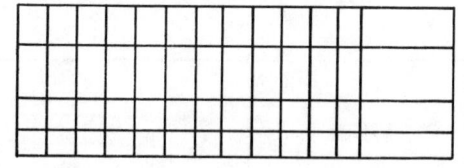

C. EVALUATION STRATEGIES   Answer yes or no and rate 1, 2, 3, 4, or 5
- Diagnostic methods are used with most or all students to determine individual reading needs.
- The teacher has formulated or selected specific objections for each student and performance is measured in terms of those objectives.
- Records of progress are kept for each Individual student's performance.
- Students are kept informed of their progress and are involved in self-evaluation (teacher-student conferences).
- Other

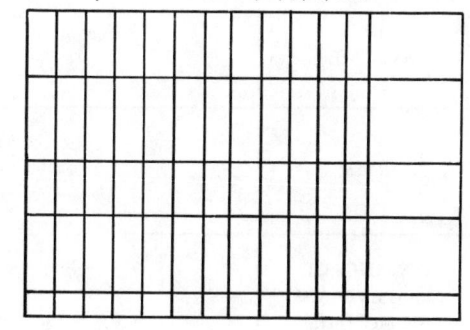

Note: Using this chart helps to review the current status of the school's existing reading program and assign priorities for improvement.

SCHOOLWIDE READING ASSESSMENT

DATA COLLECTION

GRADE OR LEVEL_____

SUBJECT OR AREA	
EVALUATION INSTRUMENT USED	
DATE	
CLASS RANGE	
CLASS AVERAGE	
NORM	
DISTANCE OF CLASS AVERAGE (IN MONTHS)	

Note: Use this form to record pertinent data so as to gain an overall statistical picture.

PROGRAM ORGANIZATION

GRADE OR LEVEL

Answer yes or no and rate
1, 2, 3, 4, or 5

RANKED PRIORITY

PROGRAM ORGANIZATION
A. Is reading taught as s separate subject?
B. Is reading taught indirectly through other subject-matter courses?
C. Is special assistance provided for students in need of special reading help?
D. Is single teacher-multi-subjects organization used in the reading program?
E. Is a reading specialist available to teach students and/or consult with teachers?
F. Is *team teaching* used in the reading program?
G. Is tutoring used?
H. Is a program in effect using a certificated teacher on a one-to-one or *small group basis*?
I. Is an *aide* available to serve as paraprofessional staff member to assist the teacher?
J. Other (Specify) _____
K. Which of the following *basic approaches* and techniques are used for reading instruction?
   - Meaning Emphasis
   - Code Emphasis
   - Linguistics
   - Modified Alphabet
   - Programmed Learning
   - Individualized Reading
   - Language Experience
   - Eclectic
   - _____

Note: Using this chart helps the committee or team view the organization of the reading program and determine what basic approaches are used for instruction.

GROUPING AND ARTICULATION

GRADE OR LEVEL

L. What student grouping patterns are used?
- One-to-one
- Small groups (5 or less students)
- Large groups (6 or more students)
- Total class
- Heterogeneous
- Homogeneous
- Is there need to study group patterns?
  Yes_____ No_____ Priority?
- Do students change groups?

Check those used:

M. What features of a *planned and articulated* reading program are evident?
- Is a single planned, systematic program for teaching and decoding skills used for most students in the school?
- .'. . . comprehension skills used for most students in the school?
- . . . study skills used for most students in the school?
- . . . vocabulary skills used for most students in the school?
- Is there an alternative program provided for individual children who need it?
- Does the teacher use the text manual and supportive materials?
- Is a written record of skills mastered by each student (basal and recreational) passed to the next teacher?
- Is a written record of each student's reading level provided for content area teachers at junior and senior high?
- Is provision made in the school for careful reading placement of the entering student who comes with no records?
- Is initial reading instruction provided in the student's first language?
- When will money be allocated for major change of reading materials?
  (date)_____

Answer yes or no and rate 1, 2, 3, 4, or 5.

RANKED PRIORITY

Note: Use this chart to examine grouping patterns and determine types of articulation of the reading program.

138

ADMINISTRATIVE LEADERSHIP AND SUPPORT

RESOURCES

	Excellent	Fair	Inadequate
RESOURCES: Staff and Materials			
Are skills of classroom teachers appropriate for needs of students?			
Are skills of paraprofessionals adequate for needs of students?			
Has the "Teacher Skills Assessment Form" been completed for each member of the certified staff? _____			
Has the "Paraprofessional Skills Assessment Form" been completed for classified instructional staff? _____			
STAFF READING SPECIALISTS			
Number available per week _____			
OUTSIDE CONSULTANTS			
Hours available per week _____			
VOLUNTEERS			
Hours available per week _____			
SCHOOL LIBRARY			
Total number of books in the library collection _____			
Does the school have at least 10 books per student?			
Does the school meet the standards for school media of the American Association of School Libraries?			
TEXTBOOKS			
Are adequate and appropriate reading textbooks available for each level of student *performance*?			
SUPPLEMENTAL INSTRUCTIONAL MATERIALS			
Are adequate and appropriate supplementary books and materials available for each level of student *performance*?			
ARE MEDIA MATERIALS AVAILABLE?			

Note: This chart looks at human and material resources in the program.

SUMMARY OF PRIORITIES (GOALS)

CATEGORY 1 Critical	CATEGORY 2 Important	CATEGORY 3 Desirable

Note: This form is for recording the goals needed in the school in order to have a comprehensive, effective reading program.

READING PROGRAM COMPONENTS

Note: As the committee or team formulates the reading plan for the school, it would be advised to review each major program component to ensure a comprehensive plan. Those aspects needing additional attention can be clearly delineated by using this form.

Components	Plan Includes	Further Help Needed	Who Assigned to Assist
Class Organization and Schedule			
Diagnosis Prescription Methods			
Instructional Approaches			
Student Motivation Plan			
Parent/Community Involvement			
Personnel Requirements			
Staff Development			
First Language Instruction			
Bilingual Instruction			
Materials			
Material Keyed to Skills			
Instructional Equipment			
Management System			
Record Keeping			
Facilities			
Per Pupil Cost			
Evaluation			

SCHOOLWIDE READING ASSESSMENT

11
STANDARDS OF EXCELLENCE FOR READING PROGRAMS

These standards of excellence were developed by the National Right to Read Program.* They have been used throughout the nation in selected school districts. As staff in schools assess their program, these standards can serve as a final step to implementation of a comprehensive reading program.

1. A comprehensive needs assessment serves as a basis of program planning and change.
2. Planning for program change is systematic.
3. A local school site planning group, composed of classroom teachers, parents, school administrators, students (where feasible) and other appropriate persons, is active in planning and monitoring the programs.

4. A variety of interested persons, including teachers, principal, representative parents, school or system reading specialists, students, and community representatives, provide input into program goals.
5. Parents participate in the development and implementation of the reading program.
6. The school board participates in policy changes related to the reading program.
7. The program, in planning and making changes, involves cultural and educational leaders in institutions of higher education; nonprofit private schools; public and private nonprofit agencies such as libraries, museums, educational radio and television; and other cultural and educational resources of the community.
8. The community participates actively in program implementation.
9. The reading program and interest in reading is supported by the school faculty, school board members, administration, parents, and students.
10. The program is guided by a comprehensive set of goals that state specific instructional objectives which have been selected by the planning group.
11. The staff provides the several types of diagnostic assessments necessary for differentiated teaching, utilizing such devices and techniques as individual reading inventories, screening or survey tests, observation, and checklists.
12. The staff provides instruction necessary for a complete reading program in which attention is given to comprehension, word recognition, and work-study skills as well as to listening.

13. Goals for the program are concerned with both cognitive and affective areas.
14. The staff differentiates the levels and content of instruction in various phases of the program in accordance with diagnostic assessments which are being made continously.
15. The staff utilizes different methods and techniques for teaching according to diagnostic findings.
16. The staff shows concern for each learner as an individual person.
17. The educational setting within which the learner is expected to develop skills in reading is conducive to optimum growth in the realization of objectives.
18. The materials of instruction are varied and appropriate to the instructional objectives of the reading program as well as to the developmental needs of the learner.
19. The staff considers the effects of environmental stress on the learner.
20. The staff shows evidence of an understanding of human behavior and the culturally diverse experience background of students.
21. The program provides diagnostic testing aimed toward identifying children and adolescents with reading deficiencies.
22. The program provides reading instruction for children and adolescents whose reading achievement is below average for their age and/or grade.
23. The principal's knowledge and skill in leadership development for reading is constantly being increased.
24. The reading specialist's knowledge and skill in leadership development for reading is constantly being increased.

25. The reading program involves periodic and systematic evaluation of its effectiveness.
26. Information used in evaluation of the learner's progress or program effectiveness comes from not one but a variety of sources and from both informal and formal techniques.
27. Reading evaluation includes an assessment of the extent to which learners use the skills they possess.
28. Teacher status in reading instruction competence and in attitudes toward reading instruction is assessed.
29. The program in reading is studied by an internal or external auditor or audit process.
30. The program provides for adequate recordkeeping and record referrals to appropriate teachers as the student progresses from grade to grade.
31. Information about the need and purpose of the reading program is disseminated to the general community.
32. The reading program disseminates to the community information about group progress in reading.
33. The program provides for systematic reporting and interpreting of individual student progress to parents or guardians.
34. Progress and results of the reading program are reported in accordance with a systematic plan.
35. The program provides teachers, aides, and other ancillary educational personnel who will be given appropriate staff development to improve their abilities to teach reading.
36. The program, where children are limited in English-speaking ability, uses bilingual educational methods and techniques.

37. Staff competencies are assessed to determine if they are adequate for carrying out the program effectively.
38. Staff development is provided to meet staff needs.

*Ideas for these criteria come mainly from two sources: Public Law 93-380 and *An Assessment Scale for Use in Examining a Reading Program*, produced by the U.S. Department of Education's Right to Read.

12 PROGRAMS AT WORK

Programs work primarily because of people. Reading methodology is secondary to the staff who implement the programs. The reading programs described in this chapter include a range of grade levels, a variety of approaches. These reading efforts emphasize prevention of reading problems. Unique features of each program are described with the teacher in mind.

The most significant factor about each program is its success in meeting the needs of previously underachieving students. In that context, they are all models worthy of examination.

High Intensity Tutoring (HIT)

Program description. The High Intensity Tutoring (HIT) method has two basic thrusts: instructional and motivational. Both thrusts are carefully designed to stimulate students individually. In the instructional program there is daily calculation of the percentage of correct responses or increased word usage and comprehension. Additionally, there are reading materials that carefully control introduction of new concepts and entail frequent review. The motivational system is crucial to student progress. Those receiving tutoring get points for progress and correct responses. These points accumulate in a "bank book" and can be redeemed for tangible rewards. Both the tutors and tutees receive points and rewards on the basis of attendance.

The High Intensity Tutoring Program establishes tutoring centers for improving reading skills. Specifically, the centers offer individualized instruction designed to develop and increase vocabulary and comprehension skills.

Students in grades six, seven, and eight are selected as participants if they are at least one year below grade level or are observed by the teacher to need tutoring.

The HIT method involves tutors, tutees, a teacher, and two teacher aides. Peer teaching is a strong aspect of the program. Tutors are selected from grades seven and eight to assist peers and sixth graders. Tutors are to reinforce correct performance and to help tutees develop grade level skills in order to become tutors. Sixth grade students needing help are given priority over students at other grade levels. Tutors selected from the seventh and eighth grades have received tutoring and understand the significance of improved performance. A small number of tutors may even be slightly deficient in reading skills, but most improve as they tutor sixth graders. All tutors and tutees meet with the teacher and aides one-half hour, four days per week.

Target group. Students from grades six and seven who perform one to five years below grade levels.

Materials. A variety of materials designed for individualized instruction are used:
- Sullivan Programmed Reading
- Kirk & Kirk Remedial Reading Drills
- Barnell Loft Reading Kits
- Dexter & Westbrook Reading Kits
- Teacher-developed flash cards and games.

Staff. One teacher and two teacher aides per center.

Cost. The yearly operating budget for the reading center is approximately $26,000, or $200 per tutee. If tutors are considered, the per-pupil cost is one-half or $100 per student. The startup cost is $5,000.

Evaluation. Significant gains have been made in reading. These gains have ranged from 1.2 to 3.7 per month for tutees on standardized tests.

Contact:
Mary J. Gebert
Director
Highland Park School District
20 Bartlett Street
Highland Park, Michigan 48203   (313) 956-0147

Upstairs School

Program description. The program's primary goal is to improve reading performance of educationally disadvantaged students.

Growth is expected in reading comprehension and vocabulary. Improved self-concept and self-confidence are also important goals.

Classroom teaching includes an open-space classroom divided into five teaching stations plus a central lounge area for individual interest reading. All participants in the program use the open-space classroom for one fifty-minute period each day. They are then programmed into either regular or special classes as needed.

During the fifty-minute period, students receive instruction in spelling, penmanship, creative writing, vocabulary expansion, oral reading, English, and remedial social studies. Students enter or leave programs depending upon their individual needs. A positive, supportive atmosphere is fostered.

The program is, in fact, a school within a school in that additional subjects include remedial math and English. For this alternative class, inservice programs are designed for the teaching staff.

Target group. High school students reading two or more years below grade level.

Materials. A variety of reading materials are used in this mastery teaching method: basic reading series, magazines, and newspapers. All textbooks are based on phonetics, and linguistic materials are used. Special interest books with high interest and low vocabulary are also used. There are teacher-developed materials as well.

Staff. A regular teacher who has special interest and skills in teaching reading and relating it to other subjects.

Cost. Title I funding averages $250 per student.

Evaluation. The California Test of Basic Skills is given each spring to all participating students. Gains in reading and language arts have exceeded the program's objectives.

Contact: Clarence A Boyer
Project Director
6941 North Central
Portland, Oregon 97203   (503) 286-5781

Proving Achievement Through Teacher and Aides

Program description. Through personalized and concentrated interaction, the problem of reading deficiency is "treated." On a one-to-one ratio for an hour a day, secondary students receive intensive instruction in reading. The instruction is based on a thorough analysis of reading deficiencies.

Emphasis is placed upon rebuilding positive attitudes and developing self-confidence. Personal interest and reinforcement are essential in developing reading interest and skills for students who have long experienced failure.

The actual reading instruction occurs within the context of the total language arts curriculum. Supplemental staff provide the extra help to students in the classroom.

Target group. High school students reading two or more years below grade level and/or students with low or failing grades in English.

Materials. All instructional and management materials used are commercially available. A wide variety, based on teacher judgment and student interests, are prescribed as needed. No particular products or systems are stressed.

Staff. A project teacher and a team of eight aides who assist students in the classrooms.

Cost. Startup cost is approximately $200 per student (based on 180 students.) This includes employing one project teacher and eight teacher aides as well as materials, equipment, and inservice education.

Evaluation. Project evaluation is based upon successful accomplishment of state performance objectives. Some 35 percent of students have gained 1.1 months per month of instruction on the Gates-MacGinitie Reading Test.

Contact:
Leon West, Director
Sky View High School Project
Cache County School District
2063 North Twelfth East
Logan, Utah 84321   (801) 752-3925

Hosts Corporation (Help One Student to Succeed)

Program description. The program focuses on human resources in the community (over 1,200 volunteers) to improve the reading levels of students. The reading curriculum is based on diagnosed individual student-reading deficiencies and modified through the use of criterion-referenced tests. Appropriate materials and activities for students help the volunteer and trained tutors who offer one-on-one instruction.

Target group. Students from kindergarten through twelfth grade as well as functionally illiterate adults.

Materials. The HOSTS project includes the Fountain Valley Teacher Support System, plus cross-referencing notebooks and a tutor training manual.

Staff. Community tutors, and student tutors for cross-age tutoring.

Cost. The startup cost ranges between $30 and $115 per student, with an ongoing cost between 50 cents to $12 per student per year for 2,000 students. The cost is flexible depending upon existing resources.

Evaluation. Both normative (achievement) and formative (individualized) tests are used. On the average, students have doubled their learning rate while in the HOSTS project.

Contact:
>Bill Gibbons, Project Director
>Hosts Corporation
>5802 MacArthur Boulevard
>Vancouver, Washington 98661 (206) 694-1705

Discovery Through Reading

Program description. Discovery Through Reading is a highly structured reading program using a Task Sheet as its core. Designed to increase the level of achievement in word recognition and comprehension, each student has an individual file of materials and tasks geared to his or her needs. The teacher works with two students at a time for a period of forty-five minutes twice a week.

During a given session, the teacher discusses with each student the tasks to be completed. As tasks are finished, a star is placed in the appropriate place on the Task Sheet. Thus reinforcement is readily available. The activities or tasks are divided into independent and dependent jobs.

Verbal interaction between teacher and student is an important part of the project. Additional materials related to specific tasks are not lumped together but spread out so that maximum benefits and reinforcement can be obtained.

Target group. Grades two and three for low-achievement students. It could be adapted to all grade levels, kindergarten through grade twelve.

Materials. Both phonetic and linguistically structured materials are used. There is a wide variety of such materials utilized in the project.

Staff. One extra teacher.

Cost. For consumable supplies and enrichment materials, the program can be started for $20 per child. The tachistoscope, SRA, or Barnell Loft Kit and other such reading materials amount to $420 per student. This excludes salaries.

Evaluation. The Stanford Reading Test and the Botel Word Recognition Test are used as before and after tests. They are given in September and May, respectively. The average student has exceeded month-per-month gains, and in many instances, students have doubled a year's growth in reading.

Contact:
Dorothy Neff
Clarkston School District
6950 Middle Lake Road
Clarkston, Michigan 43016   (313) 625-3330

Remedial Reading (Title I)

Program description. The program is direct, practical, and effective in improving reading of low-achieving students. A battery of diagnostic tests are administered to each student. Organizationally, the program is geared to small group instruction utilizing a teacher-designed remedial plan. Individual needs are addressed during a period which ranges from thirty to fifty-five minutes depending upon grade level. Each teacher develops his or her own instructional methods to meet the objectives of the project.

Target group. Students eligible for ESEA Title I, who are underachieving in reading. The program operates in grades two through nine.

Materials. The foundation of the program is the locally constructed Remedial and Corrective Handbook and Diagnostic/Prescription Summary forms as well as commercially available remedial reading materials and some teacher-developed reading materials.

Staff. Two teachers with expertise in reading.

Cost. The remedial plan costs $268 per student for 750 students. Some 93 percent of budget covers teacher salaries and fixed charges. The remaining budget covers one fully equipped remedial reading classroom in each of the two schools.

Evaluation. Data shows the mean gains have exceeded one year in vocabulary and comprehension at each grade level. The Gates-MacGinitie Reading Test is used.

Contact:
   Lorraine Curry, Assistant Superintendent
   Flagstaff Public Schools
   Title I Remedial Reading
   701 North Kendrick
   Flagstaff, Arizona 86001   (602) 779-6400

Early Childhood Education — All Day Kindergarten

Program description. This unique all-day kindergarten program has as its goals to improve language development, strengthen auditory and perceptual skills, and assist in developing the role of the family in motivating their children.

Utilizing a structured curriculum, the program emphasizes individual and small-group instruction. Diagnosis of each child forms the basis for prescription or instruction.

The classroom is organized so as to facilitate small group and individualized work with children. A central console and headphone units are significant parts of the project. A variety of manipulative materials aid in the development of perceptual skills. The additional time (full day) provides opportunity of positive reinforcement and extra instruction.

Once a month, specially designed inservice education is scheduled for teachers and teacher aides.

Target group. Kindergarten children.

Materials. Sullivan Reading Readiness and various manipulative and teacher-developed curriculum materials are used.

Staff. A regular classroom teacher and teacher aides.

Cost. Approximately $1,000 per pupil for 605 children. The program was jointly funded by the school district and ESEA Title I.

Evaluation. Within an eight-month period, the children attain "normal" reading readiness levels. The evaluation design compares children with national norms and with half-day kindergarteners. The three tests used are Metropolitan Reading Readiness, Peabody Picture Vocabulary, and Boehm Test of Basic Concept.

Contact:
    Jane Pope
    Early Childhood Education
    230 East Ninth Street
    Cincinnati, Ohio 45202   (513) 369-4720